THE EMERGING CATHOLIC UNIVERSITY

THE EMERGING
CATHOLIC
UNIVERSITY

P. H. RATTERMAN, S.J.

WITH A COMMENTARY ON THE
JOINT STATEMENT ON THE
RIGHTS AND FREEDOMS OF STUDENTS

FOREWORD BY
EDWARD JOSEPH SHOBEN, JR.

FORDHAM UNIVERSITY PRESS

NEW YORK   1968

PRINTED IN THE UNITED STATES OF AMERICA
by THE COLONIAL PRESS, INC.
Clinton, Mass.

SHORT-TITLE LISTINGS OF ORGANIZATIONS

AAC   Association of American Colleges
AAUP   American Association of University Professors
ACE   American Council on Education
ACLU   American Civil Liberties Union
JEA   Jesuit Educational Association
NASPA   National Association of Student Personnel
        Administrators
NAWDC National Association of Women Deans and
        Counselors
USNSA   United States National Student Association

Foreword

As 1968 DRAWS TO A CLOSE, the idea that change is the dominant *motif* in contemporary life is indisputable. Human creativity in the realms of science and technology has sent us hurtling into the twenty-first century, and the social correlates of inventiveness in atomic energy, electronics, and space exploration—such concomitants as the revolution of rising expectations, the manifold pressures of population growth, the consequences of mass communications and easier access to travel, and the intellectual and moral challenges to old creeds and behavioral guidelines that result from the so-called knowledge explosion—have made ours an exciting era but one of anxiety and confusion in the great domains of ethics and public policy. As inherited systems of belief and ancient patterns of value reel under the impact of modern novelties, men and their institutions struggle to adapt to change, to direct it in ways that will fulfill some heart's desire, and to harness its dynamics to society's welfare.

In a rather paradoxical fashion, the American college and university, in whose laboratories and research libraries much of the impulse for change has been generated, has been perhaps the slowest of our institutions to respond constructively to the new world it has helped so strikingly to create. Perhaps this strange state of affairs is accounted for in part by the fact that the academy has many missions, only one of which is that of education. In the fulfillment of its research obligations, in its provision of technical expertise to governments and to the industrial enterprise all over the globe, and in its training of the increasing number of professional personnel so urgently demanded by a technologized and technical society, the university has performed flexibly, imaginatively, and at a level of competence that has often approached brilliance. In its educational functions, however—in its furnishing to young people the most relevant and facilitative opportunities for their development as persons and as citizens—our academic apparatus has typically displayed not only an insensitivity to its changing circumstances, but a resistance to modification that is often bullheaded and occasionally downright savage.

The bullheadedness and savagery undoubtedly have their roots in complex sources that it is dangerous to oversimplify. It seems highly probable, however, that they partially stem from the intense duress under which some of the longest of our academic traditions now labor. In its educational role, the university has operated fundamentally as a transmitter of the cultural legacy and as an unfolder of the inner logic of its component disciplines. The rationale is the straightforward one that wisdom derives from the models the past affords and that humaneness and decency grow out of the mastery of systematic bodies of knowledge. "To know the truth is to do it," and "Know the truth and the truth shall make you free."

But the tempo, massiveness, and intimacy of contemporary social change have given a new cogency, poignancy, and urgency to Pilate's question, and it is Pilate's question that today's youth are vigorously asking. *Is* the heritage of

yesterday the best tool for dealing with tomorrow's problems? *Do* the older members of society have the insight
and ability to effectively teach the young? *Are* the values
and commitments of our forefathers the ones that define
a good life for ourselves and our children? *Are* intellect
and rationality the roads to genuine civilization, or does
recent history suggest that the cultivated brain may be the
organ of the most squalid forms of urban cruelty and
genocidal barbarism?

Such queries are radical in the best sense and intensely
legitimate in the eyes of all men who share a faith in the
interrelatedness of thought and morality. They can be
neither easily responded to nor wished away, and any bona
fide quest for suitable answers carries with it two entail-
ments: (*a*) a drastic lowering of the barriers between
those known as students and those known as teachers
because all, in the face of such issues, are students, and
(*b*) a significant enlargement of the freedom that is the
condition of such a quest.

Although it is certainly accurate to argue that freedom
is not license and that freedom requires the leaven of responsibility, the rhetoric of license *vs.* liberty and of responsible constraint can be misleading and even corrupting.
In our jumbled time of revolutionary change, the old
boundaries between academic disciplines, between campus
and community, and even between intellect and affect have
been breached beyond repair. As never before, ideas, the
stock in trade of the academy, must be tested and understood by their consequences; and the implications and
meanings of those consequences can only be effectively
sought in the most private corners of one's personal conduct
and in the most public regions of one's social involvement.
The myth of the classroom as the locus of significant learning is no longer viable, and if the goal of the examined life
is to be achieved in contemporary terms, university-based

reflection must be integratively joined to the deepest and most realistic experience of self and community. Meaningful participation and commitment are no longer proper goals of higher education; along with progressively more informed and sophisticated forms of reflection, they are necessary parts of its method. For this reason, our conceptions of academic freedom must once again be sweepingly reconceived, and that reconception must focus on the freedom of students at least as luminously as on the freedom of faculty. Because Father Ratterman's little book deals with the tough and complex problems of reconception in relation to the best ideals of the academic world and the still larger ones of our Christian heritage, it makes a singular contribution to our thinking. Addressed primarily to the Catholic colleges of the United States, its sinewy honesty and perceptiveness has large values for an audience beyond them, and its articulateness about the educational requirements of our age will prove an aid both to our youth and to those in our halls of higher learning who are responsible for their positive and productive development.

EDWARD JOSEPH SHOBEN, JR.

Center for the Study of Higher Education
State University of New York at Buffalo

Contents

THE EMERGING CATHOLIC UNIVERSITY

Introduction

DURING THE 1966–1967 ACADEMIC YEAR the author had
the opportunity to participate, as a delegate of the National
Association of Student Personnel Administrators (NASPA),
in a series of formal and informal considerations of the
document which has now been endorsed by five national
educational associations as "The Joint Statement on the
Rights and Freedoms of Students." In January of 1967 he
was asked by the Commission on Colleges and Universities
of the Jesuit Educational Association to establish a special
committee to study the implications of the Joint Statement
to Catholic higher education and also to keep the presidents
of the Jesuit colleges and universities informed with respect
to trends in student thinking that were reflected in the
Joint Statement. A series of reports were subsequently
made to the Jesuit presidents as well as to the academic

deans and student personnel officers of the twenty-eight Jesuit colleges and universities in the United States. There was nothing of a confidential nature in these reports. They were widely distributed to professional colleagues and discussed at numerous campus and regional meetings.

While this work was in progress it was suggested that a *single* article be written for the June, 1967, issue of the *Jesuit Educational Quarterly* (*J.E.Q.*) which would provide at least a partial explanation of student unrest on Catholic campuses. That single article was ultimately expanded into five articles as ideas and further considerations grew out of reports, discussions and meetings. The first four of these articles comprise Part One of this book, *The Emerging Catholic University*. The fifth article, "A Report and Commentary on the Joint Statement," is presented as Part Two.

Because an extended consideration of Catholic university education was not originally intended but only came about as the single proposed article for *J.E.Q.* was expanded into five articles, a number of explanations are in order. Chapter I, "The Context of Student Problems on the Catholic Campus," now appears somewhat dated because the manifestations of Student Power, already quite evident in the spring of 1967 when the piece was written, took a more radical turn during the spring of 1968 than was anticipated. The consideration in Chapter II grew out of discussions with colleagues on public campuses. As both public and private universities in the United States are struggling to accommodate the concept of student academic freedom to the evolving realities of campus life, perhaps it will come about that Catholic (and other Christian sectarian) universities, drawing on the wisdom of their Christian heritage, will develop an academic style and character which will actually allow a more meaningful freedom for true scholarship than public campuses will be able to provide. In other words, it seems reasonable to presume that Christianity has truths and values to offer which can prove a positive asset to an academic community aspiring to seek truth in an atmosphere of creative freedom—but only if the Catholic university conceives itself as fulfilling "A Unique Educational Mission" *within* academe. And this in turn presumes changes *within* the Catholic university itself.

The Catholic university is dreadfully afraid of change because it perceives change as a threat to its religious commitment. It has witnessed the gradual secularization of so many other sectarian colleges and universities in the past hundred years. The Catholic university wants to remain Catholic. It is pledged to retain its religious commitment whatever the cost. If it does not retain this commitment, what reason is there for its existence? Preserving Catholic commitment has through generations meant preserving an independence from the larger, and at times hostile, academe. To suggest at this point that the Catholic university adopt a unique educational mission *within* academe, and make important internal changes in order to do so, appears brash indeed. But perhaps the idea will not appear so brash when it is pointed out that the Catholic university, if it is seriously to undertake a unique educational mission within academe, far from sacrificing its religious commitment and character must deliberately seek a fuller realization of these precise qualities. What is required, actually, is only that the university now become more *catholic* while deepening all that is truly Catholic in its character.

What changes would be required if the Catholic university is to recast its educational mission so as to include a role of service within the larger academe? In Chapters III and IV it is suggested that there are five "Molds to be Broken." Chapters III and IV had to be written to explain the full implications of the unique educational mission proposed for the Catholic university in Chapter II. Most of the changes suggested in Chapters III and IV appear inevitable in view of the circumstances that are developing not only on American campuses but especially in the encompassing American society. Without doubt these changes will appear to some to constitute a threat to the very essence of Catholic education. However, what they really threaten is nothing more than a concept of religious education that is already outmoded in American society. The changes constitute no threat whatsoever to the basic religious commitment of the Catholic university. Quite the contrary: while presuming an intensification of this commitment they provide new means for its fulfillment. The changes provide for adjustments which are essential if the Catholic university is to be taken seriously in the larger academic society.

The "Report and Commentary on the Joint Statement" was the fifth of the five articles written for the *J.E.Q.* (June, 1968). Studied as a single document, the Joint Statement might appear to threaten the religious commitment of the Catholic university. However, the Joint Statement must be understood in the context of its formulation and endorsements and in this context the Statement does not constitute a threat to religious commitment but rather urges principles which are essential if the Catholic university is to play a meaningful role within the larger academe. Needless to say, there is nothing official about any of the interpretations or views expressed in the "Report and Commentary." If nothing else is accomplished in this initial effort to interpret the Joint Statement than to emphasize the idea that the Statement must be seen in the context of its formulation and endorsements, the author's main purpose will have been achieved.

Catholic universities and colleges are already currently undergoing dramatic changes. The most recent and perhaps the most startling development has been the truly revolutionary transfer of both ownership and governance responsibilities at some Catholic schools to boards of trustees which include, and in some cases are dominated by, laymen. Less conspicuous, but of far greater ultimate significance, has been the trend toward a greater freedom and increased community responsibility on the part of lay faculty and students on Catholic campuses. Philip Gleason traces the evolution which is at present occurring in Catholic higher education to social, institutional, and intellectual shifts which are occurring in American society and in the larger national academe. Gleason further feels that this evolution is solidifying around the single, basic issue of academic freedom as it pertains to both faculty and students.[1]

Considerations of academic freedom with respect to faculty and students seem logically inseparable. At the present moment the demands of student academic freedom in all universities and colleges are receiving greater public attention. Historically, however, academic freedom for faculty precedes consideration of student academic freedoms. Claims for academic freedom for both faculty and students have the same ultimate bases: respect for freedom of conscience, respect for the dignity of the individual, and respect for the respective goals of both faculty and students in the unique circumstances of the university society. The teacher must be free not just to search for truth but to teach what he sincerely believes to be true; the student must be free to seek truth in all its valid sources. In the university society dialogue and rational argument must be respected as important means to attain truth for both teacher and student. Hence freedom to speak and freedom to hear become basic rights for both student and teacher within the framework of academic freedom. These are the fundamental assertions of academic freedom in the university society as they pertain to both faculty and students.

In recent years there has been a disproportionate ferment

[1] Gleason, Philip, "The Crisis in Catholic Universities: An Historical Perspective," *Catholic Mind*, September, 1966, pp. 43-45.

on Catholic campuses with respect to student rights and freedoms.[2] There is no reason to suspect that this ferment will go away. Quite the contrary: there is every reason to believe that student agitation on Catholic campuses will increase in the years ahead. A great deal of the student unrest on Catholic campuses has reference to conditions which are internal to the university. What are the internal issues for which students on Catholic campuses are agitating? Basically, Catholic university students today are impatient with the almost exclusively passive role previously assigned them in the Catholic concept of university education. Monsignor John Tracy Ellis complains that Catholic colleges and universities have in the past been conducted "as though their main business was to serve as citadels for the preservation and protection of the faith, not as centers for cultivation of the intellect." [3]

Gleason points out that "the whole thrust of the old system was in the direction of inculcating in its students a previously arrived at synthesis of secular knowledge, intellectual skills, ethical values, and religious truths." [4] Rev. Michael P. Walsh, S.J., while President of Boston College, explained that "when Catholic colleges were established in this country there was in them tremendous emphasis on spiritual and moral formation of youth, sometimes as the very meaning of the college. Colleges were regarded by many, including educators, as seminaries." (Father Walsh further explains that such views were by no means limited to Catholic colleges.) [5]

In quite healthy reaction to the "citadel," "seminary"

[2] Williamson, E. G., and Cowan, John L., *The American Student's Freedom of Expression* (Minneapolis: The University of Minnesota Press, 1966), pp. 27-29.
[3] Ellis, John Tracy, "Contemporary American Catholicism in the Light of History," *The Critic*, June-July, 1966, p. 18.
[4] Gleason, *op cit.*, p. 51.
[5] Walsh, Michael P., "Where Church and World Meet," *Catholic Mind*, December, 1966, p. 46.

"old system," Catholic students are agitating today to be allowed to play a more determinate role both in their own education and in the affairs of the university community. With a consistency that is not always appreciated they are challenging university rules and standards which continue as vestiges of educational goals that are coming to be regarded in a far different perspective. Students are agitating for rights and freedoms which they feel appropriate to a true university.

That Catholic universities and colleges will change in the years ahead, to a considerable extent precisely as a result of student ferment and agitation, is a presumption of this discussion. The only questions to be asked, it is felt, are how much Catholic universities will change, in what direction they will tend, how much turmoil will attend the changes, and where the process will end. The questions, taken in order, become increasingly difficult. How much will Catholic universities change? Change is, of course, a relative matter depending on the present situation at individual schools. It is perhaps safe to answer that in many cases the changes, however gradual, will be almost revolutionary. In what direction will the changes tend? Precisely in the direction the students have already determined: toward a greater student freedom which will include a more determining student participation in their own total educational experience. How much turmoil will attend the changes? Very little, if the university provides active direction and leadership toward an ideal to which the entire Catholic university community can respond with intellectual integrity. Where will the process end? Rightly coordinated with other foreseeable developments on Catholic campuses, the process can well terminate with the Catholic university's assuming a new and unique role in American higher education by bringing the truths and values of its Christian heritage to the full consideration and service of academe.

It has already been noted that the contents of this book appeared originally as a series of five articles in the *J.E.Q.* Rev. A. William Crandell, s.j., Vice President of the Jesuit Educational Association (JEA), suggested the original article and subsequently prompted the expansion of the project into a series. Without Father Crandell's continued encouragement and the support of the JEA Commission on Colleges and Universities, the work would have been neither begun nor expanded.

Without doubt the deepest expression of gratitude must be extended to Rev. W. Henry Kenney, s.j., for his assistance in preparing the material which comprises Part One of this book. Father Kenney, at the time Chairman of the Philosophy Department of Xavier University, served as consultant and critic for the first four articles in the *J.E.Q.* He patiently read through the manuscripts. He questioned. He challenged. He discussed. He insisted on clarifications. At times he made things quite miserable for the author, but his many valuable suggestions have been incorporated into the present text.

Many ideas which were discussed at meetings of the special committee established by the JEA Commission on Colleges and Universities to study the Joint Statement have undoubtedly found their way into these pages without proper identification or acknowledgment. Gratitude can only be expressed jointly to the members of this group, again to Father Kenney, as well as to Rev. William J. Richardson, s.j., of Fordham University, Mr. Edmund C. Toomey of St. Louis University, Rev. Harry E. Hoewischer of Regis College, Dr. Mary Alice Cannon of Marquette University, and Rev. John A. Boland, s.j., of St. Peter's College.

Many professional associates gave invaluable assistance in preparing the "Report and Commentary on the Joint Statement." Extremely important were the suggestions of

Dr. Earle Clifford, Rutgers University Dean of Student Affairs (NASPA). Documents, information, and personal views were always readily available from Dr. Peter H. Armacost and Mr. John Gillis (AAC), Mr. Robert Van Waes (AAUP), Mr. Edward Schwartz (USNSA), and Miss Anna Rankin Harris (NAWDC).

Above all it is important to express appreciation to the many wonderful people with whom the author has been associated through the years in a succession of conferences, workshops, meetings, and informal discussions. The ideas expressed in this book, whatever their worth, are more than anything else the result of a continuous dialogue with fellow student-personnel administrators, faculty members, and students—for all of whom the author has the greatest respect and in whom he has an even deeper faith.

Xavier University
Cincinnati, Ohio

PART ONE
THE EMERGING CATHOLIC UNIVERSITY

I

The Context of Student Problems

*on the Catholic Campus**

STUDENT VIEWS AND ATTITUDES on Catholic campuses cannot be understood without some comprehension of the context in which modern student problems are developing. Catholic students do not, should not, and cannot be made to, live in isolation. Their views and attitudes are strongly influenced by the situation which prevails in the larger academe. Students in Catholic universities are very much aware of the rights and freedoms allowed students in other universities. And even though in a very real sense they are disturbed by what they regard as abuses of these same

---

* June, 1967; revised.

freedoms, they frequently envy the rights and freedoms granted other students to make mistakes and learn by experience. While they are occasionally critical of the situation on other campuses, and perhaps unduly so, they perceive much that is good in the larger academic society. They seek to achieve a recognition of these same values on the Catholic campus. Prior, therefore, to any consideration of student rights and freedoms on the Catholic university campus, a serious effort must be made to understand and evaluate the context in which Catholic university students perceive their problems. Three particular external influences are especially important to the consideration: student views of the Radical Left, the proposals of civil liberty societies for university governance, and the secular-humanist concept of academic freedom.

A. THE RADICAL LEFT

1. "The System"

In order to understand modern student views with respect to student academic rights and freedoms one must first comprehend the perspective in which the Radical Left, or New Left, views modern society. The Radical Left analysis of modern society does not fit the conventional social and political categories. In place of the usual liberal (left), center, and conservative (right) positions into which we ordinarily, and all too easily, categorize political and social views, modern students see three very different groupings. To the left is, of course, the Radical Left itself. In the conventional center the student sees the modern liberal. At the right is "the system." "The system" encompasses any social, political or religious organization which is large, affluent, organized, technical, and, above all, highly impersonal.

Grouped together, therefore, on the right are such unlikely bedfellows as big government, big business, laissez-faire capitalism, Communism and organized religion. In the liberal camp the student places persons (usually over thirty) and groups that think radical (who say they want to change "the system") but who somehow have a stake in "the system" and so cannot really be trusted. At the radical left are those who are willing to risk all (or who have nothing to risk) for the social changes that are necessary to dethrone "the system." It is an interesting perspective and in many ways far more logical than the conventional construct.

Jacques Maritain expresses a very similar position. "The pure man of the right detests justice and charity, preferring hypothetically injustice to disorder." [1] Charles Davis expressed the same thought when he stated upon leaving the Catholic Church, "There is concern for authority at the expense of truth and I am constantly saddened by instances of the damage done to persons by the workings of an impersonal and unfree system." [2] Maritain and Davis express quite precisely the complaint of the Radical Left against "the system." "The system," says the Radical Left, cannot be reconciled with justice, charity, honesty, freedom and human dignity.

During the November-December, 1966, disturbances on the Berkeley campus Chancellor Roger W. Heyns is quoted as saying that some of the agitators "are out to destroy" the university, "while others want to control it." [3] Chancellor Heyns is undoubtedly quite correct in his suspicion that some of the student agitators on the Berkeley campus really

[1] Maritain, Jacques, "Maritain Charts a Course Through Change" (an interview by John Howard Griffin), *The National Catholic Reporter,* November 9, 1966.

[2] "Davis Leaves the Church," *The National Catholic Reporter,* January 4, 1967.

[3] "Cooling it at Berkeley," *Time,* December 16, 1966, p. 110.

intend to destroy the university. It is a position of the Radical Left that any "system" which is beyond reform must be destroyed. There is little doubt that at least some Berkeley radicals consider the university so systematized and impersonal that it is beyond reform. The campus radical, it might be added, feels no responsibility to provide or even to suggest alternatives for "the system" he criticizes or seeks to destroy. "The system," he reasons, is too entrenched for there to be any danger of its immediate fall. His function, as he sees it, is forcefully to expose non-answers.

Some of the documents of the Radical Left, notably those of SDS (Students for a Democratic Society), are liable to impress the uninitiated as a hoax of some kind. "[Students and faculty] must wrest control of the educational process from the administrative bureaucracy. They must make fraternal and functional contact with allies in labor, civil rights, and other liberal forces outside the campus." [4] It is a bit disconcerting for student personnel administrators to find students being urged by SDS to "hold mock trials for the Dean of Men and Dean of Women for their 'crimes against humanity.' " [5] It is a bit difficult to realize that such statements are seriously intended. They are.

2. The University Society

Where there is a possibility of reform the campus radicals and associated liberals have their own views for university reorganization. Some absolutely secure base for student rights and freedoms must be provided. It is proposed, therefore, that the three traditional sectors of the university—students, faculty, and administration—should each be com-

[4] "Port Huron Statement," Founding Convention of Students for a Democratic Society, Port Huron, Michigan, June 11-15, 1962.
[5] Davidson, Carl, S.D.S. National Vice-President, "Toward Student Syndicalism," *New Left Notes*, September 9, 1966, p. 11.

pletely autonomous, each absolutely independent, each with an ultimate right of free decision with respect to its own particular functions in the university society. Some procedures, it is allowed, must necessarily be provided for the adjudication of problems where functions of the respective sectors conflict. It is a bit difficult to reconcile the proposed three-autonomous-sector concept of the university society with the further student claim that "student affairs" embrace every aspect of university life. That would appear to leave very little to be adjudicated between the faculty and administration sectors.

Two quite opposite views are endorsed by various student groups of the Radical Left with respect to campus government. First, there is the view that the university is not distinct from civil society and should, therefore, be governed only by the rules and regulations of the larger society.

The university is simply a part of a larger political entity. Its campus is an extension of the city streets. Its central mall is the university's Hyde Park. The city ordinances set its standards of conduct, or the permissible. The important fact about the student is that he is a citizen. The rights of all members of the university are most clearly and definitively spelled out in the U. S. Constitution. The rules that govern a student are those of a citizen in court. The university is essentially a town meeting, each citizen having one vote.[6]

The quite opposite view, that the university should not be considered responsible to civil authority, is supported by probably a greater number of the Radical Left. These would hold that the university should be regarded as something unique, inviolate and sacred, not to be interfered with by civil society in its conduct of university affairs. This view is reflected in the first of the five demands made by student strikers at Berkeley University:

[6] Heyns, Roger, "Extremes of Action Are Polarizing Our Campuses," *College and University Business*, January, 1967, p. 46.

That policemen never be called onto campus to "solve" campus political problems. (Such action is entirely inappropriate in an academic community, dedicated to rational and aware problem-solving.) [7]

There are several interesting corollaries to the three-autonomous-sector theory of university government. The proposal cannot be taken seriously, quite obviously, unless the student sector is accepted as equal with the faculty and administration sectors. It is obvious too that equal status cannot be claimed by students unless the traditional concept of student is somehow changed. The position of a "student" is, after all, by nature inferior to that of "teacher" in the traditional university concept. Such an inferior position cannot be reconciled with the equal-sector theory. The university cannot, therefore, be broken into student / teacher categories. It can only be conceived as a "community of scholars," students and faculty being equals as "scholars" (with administration reduced to mere functionaries who provide the necessary educational accommodations).

For obvious reasons the stand for equality among university sectors has difficulty allowing for any degree of immaturity on the part of students or particular student groups. The November, 1966, front cover of *Moderator,* a moderately Radical Left student magazine, caricatured any such consideration as "America's Baby Policy." Regardless of what psychologists and sociologists say, the seventeen year old entering college must be regarded and respected as fully mature and treated as such, an equal among equals in the university society.

The three-autonomous-sector concept of university society, conceived as a means to guarantee student freedoms, is unquestionably to some extent an outcome of legitimate student frustration. USNSA officers explain three phases in

[7] *Commonweal,* editorial, "As Berkeley Awaits Ronald Reagan," January 27, 1967, p. 443.

their recent efforts to attain student rights and freedoms.[8] During the 'fifties USNSA's efforts centered on a recognition of student rights, and this they feel they have reasonably achieved. At least the existence of student rights is today generally recognized. As a move toward the implementation of these rights, USNSA, during the first half of the 6os, strove for student representation on important university committees and boards. This move met with partial success. It revealed, however, a student weakness in that student delegates were frequently persuaded in meetings to accept positions which could not be reconciled with ideals for student rights and freedoms currently being advocated by USNSA.

USNSA, therefore, is now entering a third phase for influencing the university society to student views, a phase where "program" is being stressed, the purpose being to see that student delegates who are accepted as equals on university committees are properly instructed to USNSA views. The USNSA three-phase plan, as outlined above, is both responsible and appropriate to university procedures.

One cannot but wonder, however, how frustrations might express themselves if the third phase fails to bring the changes in the university society which USNSA currently proposes. Is a fourth phase, "Student Power!" to be expected? The late Dr. Martin Luther King, Jr., wrote from the Birmingham jail:

We have not made a single gain in civil rights without determined legal and nonviolent pressure. . . . We know through painful experience that freedom is never voluntarily given by the oppressor; it must be demanded by the oppressed.

The student rights movement has learned too much from

[8] AAUP, Committee S, consultation on proposed Statement on Student Academic Freedom, Washington, D.C., November 13-14, 1966.

its participation in the civil rights cause to be ignorant of
Dr. King's experience. The question is not whether student
power will become a factor in the university argument. It
already has. An evolving problem for USNSA and other
responsible student groups is not just to restrain student
power to "legal and non-violent pressure" but especially to
restrict it in such a manner that it will not destroy the
possibility of reasonable disagreement and rational argument in the university society. One is horrified at the recep-
tion given to the then Secretary of Defense, Robert S.
McNamara in November, 1966, when he was effectively
silenced on the Harvard campus. This was certainly an
exercise of student power run amuck. Student power, it
would appear, can no more be reconciled with "rational
and aware problem-solving" than police power. There is a
further even more serious problem to which student power
gives rise:

The tool which blocks the path to the mere Navy recruiter in
Berkeley and to the mere President at the University of Chicago
can block the path to the classroom door if the teacher—like
the recruiter and the administrator—in the performance of his
function happens to teach what a few militant students don't
want taught.[9]

3. Lack of Trust

Students speak a great deal today about the distrust with
which they regard modern education. "So much of what
you teach us is unreal or irrelevant," they claim. "The world
we find beyond the campus is just not the world you tell us
about. It doesn't fit into your neat categories and pidgeon
holes." "People outside are being ignored, lost and hurt
every day by 'the system.' " Education itself, the radical

[9] Stahr, Elvis J., Jr. (President of Indiana University), Indiana
University News Bureau release, February 6, 1967.

student feels, has become a servant to "the system." Worse, education has itself become just one more highly technical, increasingly impersonal, huge "system" where people are ignored, lost and hurt. Teachers, especially those over thirty, are beyond hope since they have a stake in "the system." And so in frustration young radicals in some areas have turned to creating their own free universities where courses are relevant and teachers are truly free.

The student lack of trust carries into every phase of university life. Grading is a particularly vulnerable area. Really significant educational achievement, it is maintained, cannot be measured objectively, and subjective evaluation is liable to error because of personality factors. All grading, therefore, must be abandoned. Course hours, quality points and degree honors likewise provide inadequate measures for true academic achievement. They are but a form of tyranny in the educational "system." Modern education, as currently structured, simply cannot be trusted.

This same attitude of distrust carries, of course, into the area of university discipline. The Radical Left advocates a university hands-off-student-private-life policy, the university restricting the exercise of its authority solely to the academic sphere. Any further extension of university authority is an "invasion of privacy." The Radical Left argues that students are, after all, citizens, and are therefore entitled to all the rights of other citizens. The university has no right to add restrictions by insisting upon special university behavioral standards. Since faculty and administration cannot be trusted to restrain the exercise of university authority to strict university purposes, students feel they have no responsibility to obey any rule which they themselves have not approved.

4. Appraisal

Students of the Radical Left represent the angry young men in our American society. They stir "the system" from complacency and keep the liberal honest. The radical students of our present generation may not actually have read Orwell's *1984* or Huxley's *Brave New World*, but they sense the threat that size and computer know-how constitute to human dignity and freedom. They have observed firsthand in their civil rights experiences society's warped conscience tranquilized and safekept by custom and convention. They have heard "authority" and "respect for law" extolled while being used to protect injustice and even inhumanity. The Radical Left is upset and disturbed.

Campus radicals and their liberal associates hope for "a brave new world" of their own where acceptable human behavior will not be measured to the last petty detail by conformity to rules and conventions, but where human dignity, justice, integrity and love will be the mark of respect for freer men. To anybody over thirty and, it might be suspected, to many younger people as well, this is literally a frightening ideal. Earlier generations were "brought up" in a world where a young man's success was achieved when he found "his place" in society. Society was always the accepted constant. There were rules and conventions to keep it constant. It was always there. Young radicals resent not only being expected to find "their place" but they reject modern society itself as they find it. Their ultimate goal is to form a new society where there will be no preconceived or prearranged "places." Right now, in the university community, they insist that they be allowed to play a determinate role in their own preparation for the new society. Their efforts to assume mature responsibility in the university community meet, they feel, with constant rebuff. Their frustration partially explains their present insistence that they be allowed to form and control their own autonomous sector in the university community.

For a variety of social and economic reasons there are very few full-fledged members of the Radical Left on Catholic university campuses. A fair share of Radical Left ideas, however, find their way into Catholic university communities, imported and promoted by the more activist, and frequently more intelligent, students who feel they have a role to play in the formation of the evolving new society. Their ideas are not altogether incompatible with some of the views expressed in the documents of the Second Vatican Council:

The living conditions of modern man have been so profoundly changed in their social and cultural dimensions, that we can speak of a new age in human history.[10]

The not infrequent response is to complain that student activists have lost all respect for authority. Or it might be pointed out to activist students that in the full spirit of Vatican II students should not express their minds until "they enjoy competence." [11]

But can the matter be judged so simply in the university society? Is "competence" a reasonable norm for student campus expression? Is not the campus argument, where competing ideas are frequently expressed with more bravery than wisdom, the precise forum in which it is intended that students will grow in maturity and competence? Where else are young Catholics to gain the competence, so soon to be expected of them, to play a responsible role in the formation of the "new age in human history"? If personal

[10] *The Documents of Vatican II* (Walter M. Abbott, S.J., general editor), New York: Herder and Herder, and Association Press, 1966 (hereafter cited as *Documents, Vatican II*); "Constitution on the Church in the Modern World" § 54 (p. 260).

[11] *Ibid.,* § 62 (p. 270).

meekness and campus serenity are to be supreme goals on the Catholic university campus, where are students to "grow" in their ability "to wonder, to understand, to contemplate, to make personal judgments, and to develop a religious, moral and social sense" [12]?

Would it not be more honest to say that campus activists have a legitimate role to play if they do no more than prick the conscience of educational and social complacency on the Catholic university campus? Perhaps the campus ferment the activists cause helps solve another quite different and far more serious problem which the entire Catholic university community should be probing. Why are so many students in Catholic universities so complacently unconcerned about the societal problems that surround them, including problems in the university society itself? Is an unquestioning, unprobing mind the university ideal at any time, but especially on a Catholic campus during a period when "a new age in human history" is in formation?

B. CIVIL LIBERTIES INFLUENCE

The second external influence which is important to an understanding of student views has its source in the proposals of civil liberties societies for the proper governance of the university.

In 1964 Dr. Joseph F. Kauffman, currently Dean of Students on the University of Wisconsin's Madison campus, made the following observation:

When students, supported by civil liberties groups, demand precise definitions of relationships, responsibilities, obligations, and expectations, it seems evident that the student-teacher relationship is sorely tried—*the educational relationship rup-*

[12] *Ibid.*, § 59 (p. 265).

tured—and the governance of the institution defensive and harassed.[13]

The demands for precise definitions of university relationships are cited by Dr. Kauffman merely as evidence of a "sorely tried," "ruptured" educational student-teacher relationship. Might not a further question reasonably be asked? Is it not possible that the demand for precise definitions and procedures in the university society, so strongly supported by civil liberty societies, serves not merely as evidence but as a contributing cause to campus misunderstanding? One might well wonder, for example, whether a great deal of the prevailing student distrust is not generated by an insistence on procedures which force the university to act as though neither the university nor the student can be trusted. Manifest fairness and adequate protective procedures, it might be observed, are essential to establishing and maintaining an essential mutual confidence. Excessive legalism, however, will destroy it. Is it possible that civil liberty societies, all in the cause of fair play and justice on the university campus, have become so concerned with the letter of the law that they are helping to destroy its spirit?

Is there the further possibility—and the question is asked most seriously—that the modern student-freedoms movement is not benefiting by the best and most progressive civil liberties thinking?

Anyone familiar with the present-day campus situation cannot but be impressed, for instance, with the relevance of the thinking of Carl J. Friedrich. In an article entitled, "Rights, Liberties, Freedoms: A Reappraisal," Friedrich traces the history of the civil liberties movement from its

---

[13] Kauffman, Joseph F., "Student Personnel Services: Some Questions and Recommendations," reprinted in *The Educational Record*, ACE, Fall, 1964. Originally, "A Report to the Commission on Academic Affairs of the American Council on Education."

inception during the French Revolution to present times. In his historical sketch Dr. Friedrich distinguishes between the older civil rights of independence and participation and a new third class of civil rights (and freedoms) which have been made possible only by recent developments in modern society. This third class, which he terms "rights of creation," includes "the right to social security, work, rest and leisure, education, adequate standard of living, participation in cultural life, and even to an international order securing these rights." Because of the possibility in our day of implementing these new rights for the first time in human history Friedrich speaks of the abandonment of the "state of nature," "Robinson Crusoe," "isolation" concept of freedom which has dominated civil liberties thinking for so long. He speaks of a new civil liberties ideal which he terms "effective interdependence." Effectively interdependent freedom in modern society, according to Friedrich

is to be free to share *and the sphere of independence is not primary, but a corollary of participation in the community and of contribution to it through one's creativity* [emphasis added].

As Friedrich explains, "although independence still dominates the civil liberties oratory," there has been *"a profound shift of outlook and emphasis"* within the movement.[14]

One does not find any such "profound shift of outlook and emphasis" in the civil liberties thinking which is influencing the modern student academic freedom movement. Student radicals and activists appear inspired by the more antiquated civil liberties ideals which apparently are no longer applicable even in civil society let alone in the unique circumstance of the university community. The ideal of "sharing" through "effective interdependence" and the

[14] Friedrich, Carl J., "Rights, Liberties, Freedoms: A Reappraisal." *The American Political Science Review,* Vol. LVII, No. 4 (December, 1963), pp. 841-854.

concept of freedom where "the sphere of independence is not primary" are strangely unfamiliar to the campus argument. Perhaps the truly significant contribution to the student academic-freedom movement by civil liberties groups is yet to be made.

C. SECULAR HUMANISM

The concept of academic freedom proposed by Jefferson and strongly supported by the secular-humanist forces which currently dominate modern education exercises a strong influence over students on Catholic university campuses. It is a singularly engaging concept flattering man in his highest power, his intellect. It bears the typical American trait of unlimited optimism. Truth will overcome error. Good will overcome evil. Virtue will ultimately triumph.

Inscribed in gold letters circling the dome of the Jefferson Memorial in Washington, D.C., one reads the famous words,

I have sworn before the altar of the eternal God to fight against every form of tyranny over the minds of men.

A more specific expression of the secular-humanist ideal of academic freedom can be found in a letter written by Jefferson to prospective faculty members for the University of Virginia:

This institution will be based on the illimitable freedom of the human mind. For here we are not afraid to follow truth wherever it may lead, nor to tolerate error so long as reason is free to combat it.[15]

Freedom to search for truth wherever it is to be found; freedom to follow truth wherever it may lead; complete confi-

---

[15] Barth, Alan, *The Loyalty of Free Men* (New York: Viking, 1951), p. 203.

dence that in the university argument truth will overcome error—these are the basic elements of academic freedom proposed by Thomas Jefferson which are widely endorsed today in the secular academe.

In any consideration of the effect the Jeffersonian academic ideal has had upon the modern student movement, it is very important to note that rationalism has undergone a considerable change from Jefferson's day to our own. Jefferson assumed that there was such a thing as objective truth, and that the human mind had the capacity to recognize and grasp this truth. When Jefferson stated that he had no fear of error so long as reason was free to combat it he expressed an obvious belief that truth was one thing, error quite another, and that between the two there was an objective difference which the human mind could definitely perceive. Today, ironically, secular humanism endorses a most "un-Jeffersonian" lack of faith in the capacity of the human mind to perceive an objective difference between truth and error. Historically the development is not difficult to trace. Since Jefferson's day the areas in which reason has been considered competent to perceive truth (and refute error) have become increasingly restricted. In the 19th century the empirical philosophers restricted reason to the function of accumulating and codifying into laws the facts of experience. At the turn of the century pragmatism further restricted the function of the human mind to judging only that which experience demonstrated to obtain practical and meaningful results. And with the modern dominance of scientism the capacity of reason to perceive truth is all but forsaken, for today's scientific truth is certainly vulnerable to tomorrow's scientific finding. And so from Jefferson's absolute faith in reason as a source of objective truth the modern secular humanist has come effectively to deny reason as a source of any truth. From Jefferson's belief in objective truth the humanist has turned to "subjective truth." The university world today is that of the secular city, an agnostic world, a world which in a very real sense completely denies Jefferson's faith that reason can perceive truth and refute error.

Modern student thinking with respect to student rights and freedoms in the university society—and this thinking very frequently finds its way onto Catholic campuses—all too obviously reflects the prevailing secular-humanist agnosticism. What meaning has the "pursuit of truth" in a university society which does not believe that truth can really ever be achieved? What truths are "relevant" in a university world which effectively denies the possibility of wisdom? Teaching in such a society becomes a mockery, the imposition of one man's opinion upon another, the very sort of tyranny over the minds of men that Jefferson so strongly condemned. In such an educational milieu compulsion in any form is not only an offense against freedom but a violation of human dignity. The Jeffersonian formula for campus argument is preserved, but only as an intellectual sophistication or campus rite which lacks Jefferson's firm conviction that truth would prevail over error. What remains in such a society to determine truth? Power, not truth, must overcome error. Power alone can assure freedom. It is interesting to note that the student academic-freedom movement is evolving in precisely this direction.

There is a further, far more devastating effect which secular humanism sometimes has upon Catholic students. The secular-humanist concept of academic freedom is based on the assumptions of rationalist agnosticism: the *sole* source of truth is human reason; human reason cannot perceive truth with any degree of certainty; in the final analysis the human mind cannot distinguish between truth and error. The Catholic university, quite obviously, cannot accommodate itself to such assumptions. Students in Catholic universities, as a consequence, are liable to seek an apologetic and all too simple accommodation with "the true and full academic freedom." University commitment becomes an embarrassment to be explained, where possible, as university emphasis. Further, the apology and accommodation sometimes carries over from the Catholic university to religious faith itself. Religious faith becomes something not quite respectable in true academe.

Academic life has become so much more complicated than in the old days when the Catholic "citadel" response to secular humanism would have been one of disdain accompanied by strong efforts to isolate students on Catholic campuses from such obviously pernicious and heretical views. The Deism of Jefferson would have been reason enough totally to discredit any educational philosophy he might have proposed. Each new Berkeley would have been hailed in Catholic university circles as a well deserved consequence of such Godless views. Every effort would have been made to avoid public knowledge of related, and therefore scandalous, unrest on the Catholic campus. Ecumenism, however, is the order of the day and it might well be argued that common misery remains the strongest ecumenical force to appear among men. Neither Catholic nor secular educators have a monopoly on problems of student rights and freedoms. Common discomfort is bringing all educators to an understanding dialogue with respect to student problems. The propriety, however, of Thomas Jefferson's serving as patron for an ecumenical approach to these problems might well be questioned by students. Jefferson's own record in student affairs as the first president of the University of Virginia reads like the modern student freedom movement writ backwards.[16]

The forthcoming dialogue between Catholic and secular

[16] Cf. Honeywell, Roy J., *The Educational Work of Thomas Jefferson* (Cambridge: Harvard University Press, 1931), Chapter IX, "University Government."

educators on student rights and freedoms should prove fascinating. How interesting it would be if the Catholic educators were to take the position that Catholic universities are able to adapt to educational advantage more of the original Jeffersonian ideal than secular universities are able comfortably to absorb. In a pluralistic society where educational diversity is a respected ideal, competing experience might well demonstrate that the Catholic university religious commitment, far from constituting a "tyranny over the minds of men," provides an intellectually liberating force in the academic community. The Catholic university might argue that it offers the possibility for a more comprehensive search for truth than the university "committed to non-commitment" can conscientiously allow, a more academically meaningful freedom than the secular university can consistently endorse, and a premise for distinguishing truth from error academically more sound than the secular university can comfortably provide. How strange it would be if the Jefferson memorial in Washington one day became a focus of Catholic academic pilgrimage proscribed by secular-humanist academe. Meanwhile, in the agonies shared by all university educators over student agitations, it shall remain a shrine to academic ecumenism.

The words of Pope John XXIII at the opening of the Second Vatican Council are, perhaps, not altogether inappropriate. They will undoubtedly suggest different considerations to various educators.

In the daily exercise of our pastoral office, we sometimes have to listen, much to our regret, to voices of persons who, though burning with zeal, are not endowed with too much sense of discretion or measure. In these modern times they can see nothing but prevarication and ruin. They say that our era, in comparison with past eras, is getting worse, and they behave as though they had learned nothing from history, which is, none the less, the teacher of life. They behave as though at the time of former Councils everything was a full triumph for the Christian idea and life and for proper religious liberty.

We feel we must disagree with those prophets of gloom, who are always forecasting disaster, as though the end of the world were at hand.

In the present order of things, Divine Providence is leading us to a new order of human relations which, by men's own efforts and even beyond their very expectations, are directed toward the fulfillment of God's superior and inscrutable designs. And everything, even human differences, leads to the greater good of the Church.[17]

[17] *Documents, Vatican II,* "Pope John's Opening Speech to the Council," pp. 712-713.

II

*A Unique Educational Mission**

NEW VOICES ARE BEING HEARD on the Catholic campus today and older voices heeded. Almost a century ago Newman wrote of a need for fostering "elbowroom for the mind" in the Catholic Church. Where should that elbowroom be found if not on the Catholic university campus? Michael P. Walsh, S.J., while President of Boston College, urged that,

The Catholic university should be, and must be in the future, much more than it has been in the recent past, the place where the Church does its thinking.[1]

The late John Courtney Murray, S.J., speaking at a special honors day convocation at Fordham University in the spring of 1966 defined the function of a Catholic university:

* October, 1967; revised.
[1] Walsh, *op. cit.*

. . . to live on the borderline where the Church meets the world and the world meets the Church . . . , to interpret the Church to the world and the world to the Church. The borderline is ever shifting. Our first task is to find it.[2]

Such observations reveal a rethinking and a realigning of basic values in the Catholic university's educational mission. The evolving concept is already affecting the relationship of the Catholic university to its students. Students on Catholic campuses are anticipating and in some cases are forcing changes which are not altogether incompatible with the emerging concept. In particular, students are impatient that the Catholic university assume the mien of a true university.

A. DUAL COMMITMENT

It is best to think of the emerging Catholic university as having not one but two commitments. First, the Catholic university must commit itself to the educational ideal of a true university. Secondly, at the same time it must also retain its commitment to the Catholic faith. Whether or not these two commitments can be reconciled is a matter for later discussion. It is important first to consider the nature of the two commitments.

The first commitment of the Catholic university, its commitment to the educational ideal of a true university, is that which distinguishes the Catholic university from other Catholic societies. The mission of a true university is frequently expressed as "the pursuit of truth" or "the preservation, transmission and enrichment of our cultural heritage." Since the university would consider a cultural

[2] Murray, John Courtney, S.J., "The Vatican Declaration on Religious Freedom: An Aspect of its Significance," *The University in the American Experience* (New York: Fordham University, 1966), p. 10.

heritage of value only for the truth it enshrines, the primary and basic concern of the university remains truth, its achievement, its preservation and its communication. If the Catholic university, therefore, is to fulfill its commitment to the ideal of a true university, its primary and basic concern must be truth. The expression "pursuit of truth," however, provides problems which are not just semantic. The "pursuit of truth" cannot be presumed to include truth's preservation and communication where it is denied that objective truth can ever really be achieved. In view of these difficulties "the pursuit of new truth" provides a more suitable expression of the Catholic university ideal. "The pursuit of new truth" presumes that there are truths already known which are to be preserved and communicated. It expressly states, moreover, that there is to be a quest for new truth both through a deeper understanding of truth already known and its application to new problems. Any expression which involves the achievement of new truth as the university goal is particularly apt for the emerging Catholic university. Catholic educational emphasis in the past has too often been placed almost exclusively on protecting and defending truth already known.

While the basic goal of the university community must be conceived as the pursuit of new truth, the true university assumes a complementary goal particularly with respect to students. The university must involve its students in the community's quest for new truth. In other words, in the true university students are actively incorporated into the community enterprise of seeking new truth. While the advanced function of the true university is not instruction but inquiry, instruction has an important place in the true university especially for the lower classes. The university has a serious responsibility to communicate its patrimony, its truth already known, not just for its own sake but that students may be guided to the frontiers of knowledge where truly relevant and meaningful inquiry begins. But even within the frontiers, instruction at a true university labors to present truths, accepted by the university community, in a manner which enables students to embrace these truths through personal assent as each student truly discovers them for himself in his own, personal university experience. The Catholic university community cannot, therefore, if it is to be a true university, catechize or spoon feed to students its own accepted truths. The Catholic university is unique in its presentation, in full and proper context, of those truths which are considered to be known and established by the Catholic university community. To these truths the Catholic university must seek to have its students give their own "personal assent" grounded on rational understanding.[3] In addition the Catholic university must seek to lead its students to the frontiers of these accepted truths where, aided by all secular and religious branches of knowledge, students are incorporated into truly meaningful and relevant enquiry. It is the educational mission of the Catholic university to teach students "to wonder, to understand, to contemplate, to make personal judgments and to develop a religious, moral and social sense." [4]

The second commitment of the Catholic university is to the Catholic faith. It is very important that the religious commitment of the Catholic university be understood as a commitment not of individual members of the university, or of a particular (religious) group within the university community, but as a commitment of the university precisely as a total community. Not every individual member of the university need, therefore, personally share the Catholic commitment. Non-Catholic members do not in any way

[3] *Documents, Vatican II,* "Declaration on Religious Freedom" § 3 (p. 680).
[4] *Ibid.,* "Constitution on the Church in the Modern World" § 59 (p. 265).

weaken the commitment as long as all members acknowl-
edge and respect the fact that the university as a community holds the Catholic commitment. The social, community nature of the Catholic university commitment is of
significant consequence in determining the precise responsibility which the Catholic university has for the religious
and moral development of students.

The religious and moral development of students cannot
be regarded as the primary end, or *raison d'être*, of Catholic university education. Neither can it be considered
something extra, something that the Catholic university
tries to accomplish on the side, as it were, while elsewhere
it pursues its main purpose, its quest for new truth. The
religious and moral development of students must be regarded as a means by which students are effectively incorporated into the unique character of the Catholic university's pursuit of new truth. Students can be assimilated
into the full quest for new truth on the Catholic university
campus precisely to the degree that they are knowledgeable
of the religious patrimony of the community and have
committed themselves by personal assent to its fullest realization in their own lives and in the academic mission of
the university. The Catholic university cannot, therefore,
be indifferent to the spiritual and moral welfare of its
students if it is to fulfill its responsibilities as a true university of incorporating students into its primary educational mission, its quest for new truth.

B. FAITH, A SOURCE OF TRUTH

In addition to its first commitment, to seek new truth
according to the ideal of a true university, the Catholic
university community must respect its second commitment,
that which it holds to the Catholic faith. Can these two
commitments be reconciled? Everybody is familiar with

George Bernard Shaw's contention that a Catholic university is "a contradiction." Dr. Rosemary Lauer invoked the position in the recent St. John's University turmoil. It is common enough for activist students on Catholic campuses to hold that Catholic universities can have only a Catholic "emphasis," not a commitment. A university commitment of any kind, it is argued, prejudices or makes impossible an objective search for truth. A university with a commitment, it is claimed, cannot allow freedom either to search for truth wherever it may be found or to follow truth wherever it may lead.

However strongly such arguments may be urged, the actual difficulty faced by Catholic universities in modern academe is paradoxically quite different. The Catholic university today is not disturbed by the permissiveness allowed in academe in its search for truth but rather by the arbitrary limitations which are imposed upon the search by the secular-humanistic influences which so dominate modern education. Secular humanism, in the tradition of Jeffersonian rationalism, insists quite dogmatically that the search for truth be limited to only such truths as can be achieved by reason and empirical science. The Catholic university claims freedom from any such limitation. Specifically, the Catholic university insists that religious faith be regarded as a valid and respected source of intellectual truth; the secular humanist is reluctant to accept religious faith as a source of intellectual truth. Secular humanism limits the search for truth to the natural order; the Catholic university extends the quest for truth to include both the natural and the supernatural orders.

On different planes we are, you and we, oriented toward the truth—yours, the truth of the natural order, and ours, the truth of the natural and the supernatural.[5]

[5] Pope Paul VI, Address to delegates to the Italian Society of Obstetrics and Gynecology, October 29, 1966, *Catholic Mind*, March, 1967, p. 59.

The position of the Catholic university is best explained by pointing out that its special commitment is to a religious faith, not to some special philosophy or world-view. Religious faith, the Catholic university community insists, must be accepted and respected in academe as a valid source of intellectual truth. If religious faith is not a source of intellectual truth the Catholic university is, quite obviously, "a contradiction." If, on the contrary, religious faith is a valid source of intellectual truth the Catholic university is not a contradiction and quite properly insists that religious faith be given appropriate and respected consideration in the university society. The complexities of religious faith may be difficult to comprehend. However, a rudimentary understanding of faith as a source of intellectual truth, beginning on the purely natural level, is not difficult to explain. In a lecture at Xavier University, Cincinnati, on December 5, 1966, Rev. Anthony T. Padovano cited the example of a young man telling a young girl over and over that he loves her. The problem faced by the young man is that he is unable to prove his love in an empirical manner. Yet his love, he well knows, is a fact—and a very objective fact, it might be added. He might attempt to assert or "prove" this fact by outlandish feats of chivalry, thereby giving witness or testimony of his love, but his exceptional efforts only further demonstrate the impossibility of his actually proving his love empirically. The young man protesting his love over and over is asking, in final analysis, to be believed. The response is faith, and can only be faith. (One can deceive another about his love, Father Padovano noted.) For love to be known it must be believed. When it is accepted and believed, and especially when it is returned, faith becomes a means of knowing an objective fact. It is an instrument by which the human mind achieves an intellectual truth. It is both academic and scholarly to accept faith resulting from such communication—ultimately self-communication—as a legitimate, albeit limited, source of intellectual truth. Similar arguments are currently being made for intuition and insight and even for feeling and sensing as valid sources of intellectual truth. It can only be regarded as quite arbitrary to restrict truth to that which can be proved empirically.

Religious faith is essentially no different. Religious faith too can be academically respected. Religious faith results from man's confrontation with God. God speaks to man and in His very speaking attests His love. Man replies. Love is communicated and through love intellectual truth.

[Religious language] tells of what countless men have felt. It is frequently our way of saying that life is meaningful and has some intelligent direction even if we do not perceive the whole system. Religious language is often our way of saying that there is mystery about the human person and his destiny. It speaks to that within us which finds a measure of happiness here but which senses that we are pilgrims in search of another homeland. Something about our being here is unsettled and unfinished. It remains so in spite of all we say or do. This is what religious language is talking about. It seeks to speak what the heart of man so vaguely but hauntingly feels. Religious language never says all perfectly and clearly but what it does say rings true enough to man's heart and intelligence for him to say there is something valid about it. And he admits this, century after century.[6]

The Catholic university, therefore, regards religious faith as a valid source of intellectual truth—not the source of *all* truth and not the *only* source of truth. The Catholic university regards religious faith as a source of limited truth, truth which must be brought to oneness with other truths learned from other, natural, sources.

Here, I suggest, is a task for the university which bears the name Catholic. It is to be the bearer of the new movement

[6] Padovano, Anthony T., "American Unbelief and the Death of God," Xavier University Forum Series lecture, December 5, 1966.

that will transcend the present dichotomy of sacral and secular, and it is to be the artisan of their new unity. The task is manifold, complicated, and most delicate. . . . The Council [Vatican II] has dissolved an older problematic—the differentiation of the sacral and the secular. Thereby it has installed a new problematic—the unity of these two orders of human life, achieved under full respect for the integrity of each.[7]

C. FREEDOM AND CHRISTIAN WISDOM

If it is to be allowed that religious faith is a valid and respected source of intellectual truth in the academic society, a further and much more difficult problem seems immediately to arise for the Catholic university. Can a scholar in a Catholic university seek truth wherever it may be found and follow it wherever it may lead? Theoretically the Catholic university has no problem with the Jeffersonian concepts. The Second Vatican Council repeats a religious tradition that long antedates Jefferson even though in the modern educational context it might appear to echo his voice:

. . . that all men should be at once impelled by nature and also bound by a moral obligation to seek the truth, especially religious truth. They are also bound to adhere to the truth, once it is known, and to order their whole lives in accord with the demands of truth. [8]

It is an essential part of the religious faith of the Catholic university to believe that all truth, natural and supernatural, comes from God and, rightly understood, leads to God. The Catholic university would betray its religious commitment if it did not encourage all scholars to seek and follow

[7] Murray, op. cit., p. 9.
[8] Documents, Vatican II, "Declaration on Religious Freedom" § 2 (p. 678).

truth without reservation. "Faith and reason give harmonious witness to the unity of all truth." [9]

In the practical order, however, the problem of freedom in the Catholic university cannot be dismissed so lightly. The Catholic faith is taught by the magisterium of the Church, and this same magisterium is quite definitely, by divine constitution, unified in the Church's hierarchy and the bishop of Rome. Moreover, the teaching of the Church's magisterium is reinforced by a juridical order, independent of the Catholic university, which protects the Church's teaching and regulates its observance. Can an acceptance of the Church's magisterium with its own external juridical enforcement be reconciled with freedom as it must exist if the Catholic university is to be a true university? Philip Gleason puts the problem well:

Faith does indeed mean a commitment; it does assume that there is such a thing as revelation; and it does claim that there is a sort of knowledge that is valid although it is not publicly verifiable through empirical tests. Moreover, Roman Catholicism does involve the acceptance of authoritative interpretations of the revealed Word. How all of this—and more— is to be reconciled with the principles of free inquiry is by no means clear.[10]

Miss Jacqueline Grennan, President of Webster College, Webster Groves, Missouri, is currently presiding over the secularization of Webster. Her problem has perhaps been minimized.

It is my personal conviction that the very nature of higher education is opposed to juridical control by the Church.[11]

Miss Grennan's problem does not appear as basic as that

    [9] *Ibid.*, "Declaration on Christian Education" § 10 (p. 648).
    [10] Gleason, Philip, "Academic Freedom," *America,* July 16, 1966, p. 63.
    [11] *Time,* January 20, 1967, p. 66.

pointed out by Gleason since the Church's juridical control could accommodate itself to the educational ideal of a true university. Moreover the decrees of the recent Council indicate very clearly that the Church recognizes the importance of such an accommodation. There are indications in these same decrees that the magisterium of the Church will more completely integrate its own search for truth with that of the Catholic university.

In its *Declaration on Christian Education* the Council lists as a specific purpose of the Church's involvement in the field of education,

to create for the school community an atmosphre enlivened by the gospel spirit of freedom and charity.[12]

With explicit reference to Catholic colleges and universities this same declaration teaches that

individual branches of knowledge [should be] studied according to their own proper principles and methods, and with due freedom of scientific investigation.[13]

In the *Constitution on the Church in the Modern World,* where principles for the necessary and rightful independence and autonomy of secular societies are outlined, the Council strongly affirms

the legitimate autonomy of human culture and especially of the sciences. . . . Within the limits of morality and the general welfare, a man [must be] free to search for the truth, voice his mind, and publicize it.[14]

Elsewhere, in the same constitution, one reads:

Now, many of our contemporaries seem to fear that a closer bond between human activity and religion will work against the independence of men, of societies, or of the sciences.

[12] *Documents, Vatican II*, p. 646.
[13] *Ibid.*, p. 648.
[14] *Ibid.*, p. 265.

If by the autonomy of earthly affairs we mean that created
things and societies themselves enjoy their own laws and values
which must be gradually deciphered, put to use, and regulated
by men, then it is entirely right to demand that autonomy.
Such is not merely required by modern man, but harmonizes
also with the will of the Creator.[15]

In spite of the fact that the quotations taken from the *Constitution on the Church in the Modern World* deal directly
with secular societies, in the context of the entire Vatican
II proclamation they have an obvious relevance to the
Catholic university. There is the repeated reference to
"freedom" and "autonomy" for the sciences. "Scientific investigation" is the everyday business of the Catholic university. The only restrictions which the Council sees for
men seeking truth are "the limits of morality and the general welfare." The Council directs the search for truth particularly to the Church itself. "All men are bound to seek
the truth, especially what concerns God and His Church,
and to embrace the truth they come to know, and to hold
it fast." In view of such statements John Courtney Murray
explained that theology is not to return "to its pre-conciliar
state, in which the theologian had been forced to abdicate
his high function and to become simply a commentator on
the latest magisterial utterance." [16] Pedro Arrupe, S.J., applies the Conciliar spirit even more directly to the Catholic
university explaining that its perennial task is "to insure
the awareness, the talent, and the instruments whereby the
body corporate of Christianity is to do its thinking, bring
its faith to self-reflective understanding, and devise appropriate lines of action in and upon both the Church and
the world." He considers the Catholic university the

[15] *Ibid.*, p. 233.
[16] Murray, *op cit.*, p. 1.

Church's "most appropriate organ . . . of self-study and self-reflection." [17]

If Fathers Murray and Arrupe correctly interpret the mind of Vatican II, the Council obviously provides for a more complete integration of the Catholic university into the work of the magisterium itself. The function of the Catholic university is not to be confined to preserving and communicating truth as predetermined by the magisterium. It is to participate in the magisterium's own quest for new truth by reflecting the thinking of "the body corporate of Christianity." Because of its close relationship to the Church's magisterium the Catholic university shares the responsibilities of the Church, particularly of its magisterium. Within the Church it must be allowed to "enjoy [its] own laws and values which must gradually be deciphered." Only under such conditions can it function as a true university and properly serve the magisterium.

The limited freedom of the Catholic university appears as but another contradiction to the secular humanist who insists that absolute freedom is the only acceptable ideal in the true university. To the secular humanist the university must be the most free of all societies and the scholar the most free of all men. Only the man who is absolutely free can seek truth wherever it may be found and follow it wherever it may lead. Any limitation of freedom is unreasonable for the academic mission. The Catholic university can only ask in reply: Is there such a thing as absolute freedom in academe? Is absolute freedom compatible with the university mission, let alone its ideal? Does integrity limit freedom? Do responsibilities limit freedom? Does truth itself once it is perceived limit freedom? Is not absolute freedom in academe a myth?

[17] Arrupe, Very Rev. Pedro, S.J., "The University in the American Experience," *The University in the American Experience*, p. 26.

It is interesting to consider some of the concepts of freedom more commonly discussed on campuses and to speculate to what extent they provide for absolute freedom in the academic context. Freedom conceived as "the absence of external restraint" proves most inadequate. A man of strong prejudice, uncontrolled ambition or violent emotion, although not limited by external restraint, is academically not free. He is incapable of seeking and following truth. Freedom in the academic sense demands a great deal more than an absence of external restraint. It is sometimes proposed in the campus argument that the university society can allow but a single limitation to absolute freedom. Men must always respect the rights of other men. Measuring allowable limitations to freedom by the rights of others, however, provides its own strange contradiction. Freedom diminishes, it appears, as men become more aware of the dignity and rights of others. Ironically, it is the educational mission to awaken this awareness—and so diminish freedom. Freedom must be made of better stuff. These are "Robinson Crusoe," "isolationist" concepts of freedom which exaggerate individualism. They have been appropriated from civil liberties proposals which are inadequate today even for civil society. A concept of freedom appropriate to the academic community certainly demands a great deal more.

Any concept of freedom which appears suitable and appropriate for the academic society necessarily involves some limitations of absolute freedom. These limitations, paradoxically, actually promote academic freedom rather than limit it. The individual scholar, for instance, must have a style or character which frees him from disorders that limit intellectual understanding and honest judgment. In other words, to be academically free the scholar must be humble, receptive to the ideas of other men, always seeking to correct and clarify his own thinking by searching for some new truth in each new idea. He cannot be selfish, a man who "fights truth" because he is unwilling to assume its responsibilities. The academic community itself, if it is to foster a spirit of freedom appropriate for a university, must have its own internal style and character. Communication, so essential to the academic society, must be such as leads to mutually creative self-fulfillment. There is no place in the academic community for communication which frustrates a creative cooperation in the search for truth.

When the paradoxical "limiting" qualifications for the scholar and the academic community are examined it appears not only that absolute freedom is a myth but that seeking truth in an academic community presupposes that a great deal of wisdom or truth is already known. In many ways the academic community must already know and be living truth before it can be free creatively to seek new truth. And precisely here the faith commitment of the Catholic university can prove an advantage. The intellectual truth acquired through religious faith, understandingly applied to the university mission, can yield a wisdom which is peculiarly apt for seeking further truth. If the "laws and values which must gradually be deciphered" for the emerging Catholic university reflect true Christian wisdom they can provide a freedom in which individualism will be neither lost nor exaggerated, a freedom in which the academic community will be regarded as an asset to the quest for new truth rather than a liability hindering the search. There is a peculiar academic propriety in the Vatican Council's associating freedom with charity. Jesus, who so stressed the love we must have for one another, said that *His truth* would make us free. Love, truth and freedom, therefore, are interdependent in Christian thinking.

The ideals of freedom proposed for the academic society by secular humanism provide an interesting contrast with those evolving in the contemporary Catholic university.

Neither solution, as presently understood, offers a complete answer to all the problems of freedom encountered in the university society. Both lead to difficulties which cannot, with academic honesty, be overlooked. The secular-humanist concept can break down all too easily into academic anarchy. The Catholic concept is all too prone to paternalism and authoritarianism. The secular-humanist ideal of freedom for academe tends towards individualism. The Catholic ideal is likely to favor the society at the expense of the individual. Both have a great deal to learn from the other.

The situation of the Catholic university at the present time is well expressed by Gleason. First he offers two non-answers. The Catholic university cannot simply insist that things remain as they always have been, that freedom in the academic society be made "to fit into the interstices of a paternalistic and authoritarian Catholicism." Nor can the Catholic university accept "the most doctrinaire, ideological sort of freedom," currently proposed by secular humanism, as "the only true variety" for the academic society. If the Catholic university cannot accept either of these alternatives it must work out its own really creative third possibility. This, Gleason points out, will be "infinitely more laborious" than accepting either of the two non-answers he outlines, "but it will be infinitely more rewarding." [18]

D. A MESSAGE TO MEN OF THOUGHT AND SCIENCE

It is impossible to understand student unrest on the Catholic university campus today except in terms of the dichotomy presented by Gleason. Students are disturbed by the efforts of Catholic university administrators to fit the freedom which a true search for new truth requires "into the interstices of a paternalistic and authoritarian Catholi-

[18] Gleason, "Academic Freedom," p. 63.

cism." They all too frequently see the secular-humanist concept of freedom as the only alternative, "the only true variety" of freedom possible for the true university. They but vaguely understand the possibility of an emerging Catholic university offering "an infinitely more rewarding" third possibility. However, new laws and values are already gradually being deciphered which provide for the Catholic university a function within the Church with full respect for the academic mission of a true university. The Second Vatican Council provides a spirit for such new laws and values by identifying itself with true scholars.

In a remarkable document, issued in the name of the Fathers of the Second Vatican Council on December 8, 1965, at the close of the ceremonies marking the end of the Council, eight messages were addressed to various groups. One of these messages, addressed "to Men of Thought and Science," is of importance to the concept of the emerging Catholic university. In their Message "to Men of Thought and Science" the Council Fathers first explain their "special greeting": "because all of us here, bishops and Fathers of the Council, are on the lookout for truth." They point out that the work of the Council for four long years has been "a more attentive search for and deepening of the message of truth entrusted to the Church and an effort at more perfect docility to the spirit of truth." "Your road is ours," the Council Fathers exclaim, identifying themselves with other searchers for truth as "friends," "companions," "admirers," and at times "consolers." The Council offers encouragement to all of academe:

Continue your search without tiring and without ever despairing of the truth. Recall the words of one of your great friends, St. Augustine: "Let us seek with the desire to find, and find with the desire to seek still more." Happy are those who, while possessing truth, search more earnestly for it in order to renew it, deepen it, and transmit it to others. Happy also are those who, not having found it, are working toward it with a sincere heart. May they seek the light of tomorrow with the light of today until they reach the fullness of light.[19]

The message concludes with words, addressed to all academe, which have a special relevance "to Men of Thought and Science" who search for truth in Catholic university communities. "Without troubling your efforts, without dazzling brilliance," the Council Fathers offer to assist men who search for truth with "the light of our mysterious lamp which is faith."

Never perhaps, thank God, has there been so clear a possibility as today of a deep understanding between real science and real faith, mutual servants of one another in the one truth. Do not stand in the way of this important meeting. Have confidence in faith, this great friend of intelligence. Enlighten yourselves with its light in order to take hold of truth, the whole truth. This is the wish, the encouragement, and the hope, which, before disbanding, is expressed to you by the Fathers of the entire world assembled at Rome in Council.[20]

In this brief message the Council Fathers provide a general outline of the new norms and values which are to characterize the emerging Catholic university. The message indicates the special assistance the Church seeks to provide for, and receive from, all scholars in the quest for truth. Members of Catholic university communities, as men and women of thought and science, may take special guidance from the message. They are to seek truth everywhere, in both the sacral and secular spheres. They are to unite their efforts as "friends" and "companions" with all men who "with a sincere heart" are also searching for truth. They are to seek especially a unity in truth. Truth is their special mission.

[19] *Documents, Vatican II*, p. 731.
[20] *Ibid.*

They are "to renew it, deepen it, and transmit it to others." They are to have a "confidence in faith" as a "great friend of intelligence." In "the light of the mysterious lamp which is faith," a light which will provide a vision of Christ and Christian wisdom, they are to search for truth with a Christian sense of dignity and freedom.

III

*Molds to be Broken**

UNDER THE INSPIRATION of the Second Vatican Council
the broad outlines of a new Catholic university are per-
ceptibly emerging. These outlines fit neither into the interstices of a paternalistic and authoritarian Catholicism nor
are they accommodated to a doctrinaire, ideological concept
of freedom. Laws and values are being deciphered, put to
use and regulated in a way whereby the Catholic university
will be able not only best to serve the Church but to find a
respected place in academe. It is all happening and by no
means gradually. Details of the outcome are not yet certain.
However, the broad outlines of a solution are clearly developing. Both the Church and the Catholic universities are,
moreover, reacting to the change with an unforeseeable
calm and equanimity.

* January, 1968; revised.

Within the past few years several things have occurred which would have been not only impossible but unthinkable just ten years ago. The Curran affair at Catholic University in the spring of 1966 provides an instance. A faculty and student body, united by a common ideal and acting with remarkable self-discipline, forced the board of trustees to reconsider and publicly rescind their previous decision to remove Father Curran from the faculty. Many things are remarkable about the incident. Not so long ago neither faculty nor students in an American Catholic university would have thought of publicly disputing a decision expressed in the name of so many cardinals, archbishops and bishops. In 1967 the faculty-student action appeared unavoidable if they were to retain their academic self-respect. Formerly such a board of trustees would have been concerned at all costs to reflect a common front. During the Curran affair, public differences in hierarchical opinion were taken for granted even by the members of the hierarchy themselves. In an earlier day such an action on the part of students and faculty would have been thought a manifestation of a deeper, underlying anti-clericalism. In 1967 the action was neither intended nor considered to manifest any such attitude. The issue was met, settled, and by the end of the year largely forgotten without loss of faith, face or dignity on either side. The issue was clear: authority shall not act in an arbitrary manner in the university community. That settled, everybody at Catholic University resumed the more pressing everyday business.

In July, 1967, twenty-six of the best-known Catholic educators in the country, including high-ranking officers from some of the largest Catholic campuses, signed a statement which reads in part:

To perform its teaching and research functions effectively, the Catholic university must have a true autonomy and academic freedom in the face of authority of whatever kind, lay or clerical, external to the academic community itself. To say this is simply to assert that institutional autonomy and academic freedom are essential conditions of life and growth, and indeed of survival, for Catholic universities as for all universities.[1]

Such a declaration would have been unthinkable by Catholic university representatives a decade ago. What is remarkable in 1967 is not so much that the statement was made by so many leading Catholic educators but that it caused so little comment in either the secular or religious press. It was not intended as an affront to the hierarchy or, evidently, considered by the bishops to constitute an unwarranted declaration of independence. Although the precise extent, or even intent, of "institutional autonomy" is not clear, there appears a realization on all sides that this is the direction in which Catholic universities must tend if they are to function as true universities.

Rev. Leo McLaughlin, s.j., President of Fordham University, states that "Fordham will pay any price—break any mold—in order to achieve her true function as a university." [2] In the realm of student affairs, what molds must be broken, or prices paid, if the Catholic university is to perform a respected function in academe?

A. "THIS IS A 'PRIVATE' UNIVERSITY"

The first mold to be broken in student affairs is that as a private institution the Catholic university can conduct its internal student business pretty much as it pleases. Statements such as the following were not infrequent in both

[1] "Statement on the Nature of the Contemporary Catholic University by Members of the North American Region of the International Federation of Catholic Universities, meeting [at Land O' Lakes, Wisconsin] July 21 through July 23, 1967." (In mimeographed form; commentary in *America*, August 12, 1967.)

[2] McLaughlin, Leo, S.J., "Fordham in Transition," *Fordham*, September, 1966.

public and private school catalogues until the very recent past and can perhaps still be found:

The college reserves the right to exclude at any time students whose conduct or academic standing it regards as undesirable.

Or, still more explicitly:

The university reserves the right and the student concedes the university the right to require the withdrawal of any student at any time for any reason deemed sufficient to it, and no reason for requiring such withdrawal need be given.

As late as 1957 the Massachusetts State Court upheld the right of Brandeis University to dismiss students without a hearing:

The problem of what constitutes an appropriate reason must clearly be left to those authorities charged with the duty of maintaining the standards and discipline of the school. . . . I hold as a matter of law that the defendant [university] is not required to [hold any hearing before dismissing a student].[3]

Since 1957, however, several factors have entered the educational picture which make it increasingly unlikely that private universities will be allowed to continue conducting their student affairs in a manner which gives even the appearance of arbitrariness, at least where suspension and dismissal are at issue. Basically, this has come about because it is now being urged by some that a college education should be considered a right rather than a privilege in our American society.

There is a growing opinion in the United States that every young person has a right to the opportunity of a

[3] Van Alstyne, William W., "Student Academic Freedom and the Rule-Making Powers of Public Universities: Some Constitutional Considerations," *Law in Transition*, Winter, 1965, p. 4. Quoting Dehaan v. Brandeis University, 150 F. Supp. 626, 627 (D. Mass. 1957).

college education. A university education would be, in Dr. Friedrich's classification, a further refinement of the new third class of civil rights. The argument is that in our evolving American society a young person who is deprived of a college education does not have a chance to achieve the other evolving civil rights—security, work, rest, leisure, adequate standard of living, and participation in cultural life.[4] Dr. William Van Alstyne, Professor of Law at Duke University, having in mind the national welfare as well as personal need, anticipates that the courts will soon adopt an attitude toward university education similar to that which they have already expressed toward primary education. In earlier court decisions, he explains,

. . . the opportunity to acquire a university education was not widely regarded as a significant opportunity of substantial national importance. As a consequence, the courts could scarcely be expected to become exercised in reviewing the bases employed by colleges to restrict a seemingly unimportant personal privilege. Currently, however, the personal and national significance of university education enjoys unprecedented recognition. We have come to realize that the opportunity to learn in association with an academic community has enormous value for the student as an individual and for the nation as well. The right to enter into and to maintain that association is valued first of all for its intrinsic opportunities: the pursuit of knowledge, individual self-fulfillment, growth, and expression. Brigaded with these are extrinsic opportunities: to acquire useful professional skills indispensable to employment which is itself self-fulfilling and sufficient to provide an income necessary to meet one's other basic interests in food, shelter, family and leisure. . . . It is increasingly likely that [in the absence of] college preparation, employment itself becomes a remote, risky, and short-lived prospect. What the Supreme Court observed in the field of primary education a decade ago is equally applicable today at the university level:

[4] Friedrich, *op. cit.*, pp. 841-843.

"In these days, it is doubtful that any [person] may reasonably be expected to succeed in life if he is denied the opportunity of a [college] education." [5]

No court of law has gone so far as to say that any or all young Americans have a *right* to a university education. The courts have, however, definitely determined that once a student has been admitted to a public college or university, he has a constitutional right that with respect to disciplinary matters the educational opportunity shall not be interrupted or terminated by school authorities without procedural due process. Moreover, this constitutional right to procedural due process can neither be signed away by a student entering a public college or university nor abrogated by any university or state provision to which all entering students must subscribe.[6] In 1961 a U.S. Court of Appeals, reversing an earlier U. S. District Court decision, required that John Dixon and five fellow students be reinstated at Alabama State College because they had been dismissed without procedural due process:

The precise nature of the private interest involved in this case is the *right to remain* at a public institution of higher learning in which the plaintiffs were students in good standing. It requires no argument to demonstrate that education is vital and, indeed, basic to civilized society. Without sufficient education the plaintiffs would not be able to earn an adequate livelihood to enjoy life to the fullest, or to fulfill as completely as possible the duties and responsibilities of good citizens.[7]

The fifth Circuit Court in this instance reflected the indignation expressed by Harvard's Professor Warren A. Seavey four years earlier:

[5] Van Alstyne, "Student Academic Freedom," pp. 6-7.
[6] Dixon v. Alabama State Board of Education, 294 F 2d 150, 157, 5th Cir., cert. denied, 368 U.S. 930 (1961). "The State cannot condition the granting of even a [State-conferred] privilege."
[7] Dixon v. Alabama, 1961, p. 157.

It is shocking that the officials of a state educational institution, which can function properly only if our freedoms are
preserved, should not understand the elementary principles of
fair play. It is equally shocking to find that a court supports
them in denying to a student the protection given to a
pickpocket.[8]

The effect of the Dixon (2–1) ruling cannot be overestimated. In 1963 a federal district court in Florida stated
that the Dixon decision provided "the most current, explicit
and applicable statement of law governing the· disposition
of this [a similar] case." [9] A comment in the *St. Louis University Law Journal* of 1966 observes: "It seems clear that
the Dixon decision is now recognized by the federal courts
as the law of the land." [10, 11]

The Dixon ruling applies explicitly only to public colleges and universities. What will its effect be on private institutions? In the Dixon decision the court explicitly noted
that "private associations have a right to obtain a waiver
of notice and hearing before depriving a member of a valuable right." [12] Nevertheless, it is most unlikely that today any
state or federal court would sustain the Brandeis position

[8] Seavey, Warren A., "Dismissal of Students: Due Process," 70
Harvard Law Review, 1957, p. 1407.
[9] Due v. Florida A. & M., 233 F. Supp., 396, 400 (N.D. Fla.
1963).
[10] Comment, 10 *St. Louis University Law Journal,* 1966, p. 548.
[11] In view of its undoubted importance to the law as it touches
university disciplinary procedures in the future, it is interesting
to note the following observation in the Dixon decision. After
outlining a few basic procedures to insure "fair play," the court
adds: "This is not to imply that a full-dress judicial hearing, with
the right to cross-examine witnesses, is required. Such a hearing,
with the attending publicity and disturbance of college activities,
might be detrimental to the college's educational atmosphere and
impractical to carry out. Nevertheless, the rudiments of an adversary proceeding may be preserved without encroaching upon the
interests of the college" (Dixon v. Alabama, 1961, p. 159).
[12] Dixon v. Alabama, 1961, pp. 157-158.

of 1957 whereby a private university could dismiss a student without a hearing. It may reasonably be anticipated that in the future the courts will apply the same norms for due process to private and public universities alike for the following reasons: in our American society dismissal from any university carries with it a stigma of life-long consequence; dismissal from a private institution quite often effectively denies the possibility of all future education because of the admission policies at public universities [13]; the educational investment (academic credit and professional preparation) is frequently non-transferable; since private schools are performing a public function they should be required to meet state requirements where fundamental rights are concerned; private schools receiving state assistance in any form are especially bound by court requirements for public schools.

Seavey strongly questions the past position of the courts which have allowed that students could be dismissed from a private university without explanation. He claims this to be a departure "from the usual rule of contracts which requires one terminating a contract for breach to justify his action." [14] An extensive comment in a recent issue of *The Yale Law Journal* argues:

What is less clear is the application of constitutional safeguards, substantive and procedural, to "private" schools. The involvement of these schools in quasi-governmental activity, the public importance of their function, and their frequently close association with state and federal government, raises the possibility of an extension of constitutional doctrines by "paraconstitutional" techniques such as have been used in other areas of

[13] "Indeed, expulsion may well prejudice the student in completing his education at any other institution" (Dixon v. Alabama, 1961, p. 157).

[14] Seavey, *op. cit.*, p. 1409.

the law to proliferate the purpose of constitutional doctrines.[15]

The following citation is interesting in this regard. Although the opinion was overruled in 1962 by a higher court it probably reflects the thinking of the future with respect to private universities:

At the outset, one may question whether any school or college can ever be so "private" as to escape the reach of the Fourteenth Amendment. . . . No one any longer doubts that education is a matter affected with the greatest public interest. And this is true whether it is offered by a public or private institution. . . . Clearly, the administrators of a private colloge are performing a public function. They do the work of the state, often in the place of the state. Does it not follow that they stand in the state's shoes? And if so, are they not then agents of the state, subject to the constitutional restraints on governmental action? [16]

Will, therefore, private as well as public universities be challenged in the future with respect to the procedures with which they handle cases involving suspension and dismissal? The following comment probably gives the answer:

It is submitted that many of our private universities today realize that the distinction between public and private, though still accepted, rests only upon highly technical constitutional considerations and, therefore, that they must be very careful to conform to the procedures the courts have demanded of public colleges and universities in expulsion cases.[17]

At least with respect to suspensions and dismissals private universities can no longer say, "because we are a private

[15] Comment, "Private Government on the Campus—Judicial Review of University Expulsions," 72 *Yale Law Journal*, June, 1963, p. 1381.
[16] Comment, 10 *St. Louis University Law Journal*, 1966, p. 546. Quoting Gillory v. Admin. of Tulane University, 203 F. Supp., 855, 858-859 (E.D. La. 1962).
[17] *Ibid*, p. 547.

institution we can conduct our dealings with students any
way we like." It would be strange indeed if Catholic universities would feel any misgivings in this regard. Regarding
due process, John Courtney Murray wrote:

What comes to the fore today is the need that the corrective
or punitive function of authority should be performed under
regard for what is called, in the common-law tradition, "due
process." The demand for due process of law is an exigence
of Christian dignity and freedom. It is to be satisfied as
exactly in the Church as in civil society (one might indeed
say, more exactly).[18]

B. "HOW WOULD PARENTS HANDLE THIS?"

While it is reasonable to expect that in the future the
courts will insist that in suspension and dismissal cases private as well as public universities follow procedures which
adequately insure "fair play," it is less likely that the courts
will question substantive issues with respect to private
school policies and standards. The courts give every indica-
tion that they will continue to respect the right of the
private university to establish its own distinctive educational philosophy and goals, provided the educational philosophy and goals, as well as any distinctive standards and
policies, are clearly enunciated in university catalogues
and handbooks. However, it is important to note that the
legal basis upon which courts will continue to support institutional diversity in higher education is rapidly shifting.
In this instance the mold to be broken on Catholic campuses involves the theory, long upheld by the courts, that a
university exercises its authority *in loco parentis.*

Many court decisions can be cited upholding the *in loco
parentis* view:

[18] Murray, John Courtney, S.J., "Freedom, Authority, Community," *America,* Dec. 3, 1966, p. 740.

College authorities stand *in loco parentis* concerning the physical and moral welfare, and mental training of pupils, and we are unable to see why to that end they may not make any rules or regulations for the government or betterment of their pupils that a parent could for the same purpose. Whether the rules or regulations are wise, or their aims worthy, is a matter left solely to the discretion of the authorities, or parents as the case may be.[19]

. . .

As to the mental training, moral and physical discipline, and welfare of pupils, college authorities stand *in loco parentis* and in their discretion may make any regulation for the government which a parent could make for the same purpose.[20]

Even as late as 1957, the Brandeis University decision, already noted, appeared to uphold the *in loco parentis* concept.

Again, however, educational circumstances are changing. In the fall of 1966, *Time* magazine observed that "at U.S. universities this fall *in loco parentis* is suffering from rigor mortis." Van Alstyne quotes a letter from Professor Henry Steele Commager which helps to put the matter into historical perspective:

In loco parentis was transferred from Cambridge to America, and caught on here even more strongly for very elementary reasons: College students were, for the most part, very young. A great many boys went up to college in the colonial era at the age of 13, 14, 15. They were, for most practical purposes, what our high school youngsters are now. They did need taking care of, and the tutors were *in loco parentis*. This habit was reinforced with the coming of education for girls and of coeducation. Ours was not a class society. There was no common body of tradition and habit, connected with membership in

[19] Gott v. Berea College, 156 Ky. 376, 379, 161 S.W. 204, 206 (1913).
[20] Stetson University v. Hunt, 88 Fla. 510, 516, 102 So. 637, 640 (1924).

an aristocracy or an upper class, which would provide some assurance of conduct.

All of this now is changed. Students are 18 when they come up, and we have a long tradition with co-education from high school on. Students marry at 18 and 19 now and have families. Furthermore, we have adjusted to the classless society and know our way about. Therefore the old tradition of *in loco parentis* is largely irrelevant.[21]

Van Alstyne also observes that "when apologias of *in loco parentis* were tentatively offered in defense of university restrictions at Berkeley in 1964, a hasty retreat was taken when it was pointed out that the overwhelming majority of students were more than twenty-one years of age." [22]

Court decisions in very recent years do not support the *in loco parentis* position. The Dixon and Due decisions of 1961 and 1963 made explicit reference to the students' "right" to remain in a public institution of higher learning where they were in good standing. In so ruling the courts introduced a consideration which is difficult to reconcile with the *in loco parentis* concept of university administration. The *coup de grâce* for the *in loco parentis* theory of college and university government, at least for state schools, was administered by the state courts of California in their judgment of a case arising out of the Berkeley disturbances of 1965. Four students, of whom one, Arthur L. Goldberg, had been dismissed, and the other three suspended, sought reinstatement to the University of California through the courts. The ruling of the California Court of Appeals in the Goldberg case, unanimously affirmed by the California Supreme Court, will probably become basic to American law in the years ahead. The court refers to the University's "inherent general powers" as the basis of the authority

[21] Van Alstyne, William W., "Procedural Due Process and State University Students," 10 *UCLA Law Review*, pp. 377-378.
[22] Van Alstyne, "Student Academic Freedom," p. 17.

which the public university exercises as a "constitutional department or function of state government." The court explicitly states that, "for constitutional purposes, state universities should not stand *in loco parentis* to their students." [23]

Although the Goldberg ruling explicitly pertains only to state universities, there are good reasons why the *in loco parentis* theory of university authority should be discarded in all private as well as public schools. Catholic universities may be more inclined than other private schools to attempt to retain the *in loco parentis* concept in view of the strong position taken by the Church with respect to parental rights in education. For instance, the Second Vatican Council insists that parents "must be acknowledged as the first and foremost educators of their children," and while the Council recognizes the duty of society to promote education in many ways, it insists that society must complete the task of education "with attention to parental wishes." [24]

Nevertheless, a Catholic university's first obligation must be to function as a true university, and this must be presumed to be the "parental wish." Moreover, the authority by which a Catholic university fulfills its tasks is not delegated by parents but is "inherent" in the university by virtue of its charter. In addition, academic and behavioral standards for students cannot be determined by family practices but must be determined by university authority according to the needs of students *as members of an academic community*. It may well happen that a private university,

[23] Goldberg v. Regents of University of California, 57 Calif. Reporter, 463, 464-5, April, 1967. It is interesting to note that in this decision a college education is defined as a state "important benefit" of which students in good standing may not be deprived without procedural due process. The Dixon and Due cases are cited as precedents.

[24] *Documents, Vatican II*, "Declaration on Christian Education" § 3 (pp. 641-642).

because of its particular educational goal, insists on student behavioral standards (by virtue of its own authority) which are not only appropriate and necessary to the academic community but which are also very much in accord with "parental wishes." The two ideals are, after all, not incompatible. The important point is that the *immediate* norm for Catholic university student behavioral standards can never be "parental wishes" but must always be the needs of students as members of a Catholic university community. It is difficult to see how a university acting on its own inherent authority and establishing standards which are appropriate and necessary for its own educational goals is acting *in loco parentis* even though "parental wishes" are being served.[25]

What is, then, the relationship of a university to its students? With the abandonment of *in loco parentis* as the basis of university government it is not to be presumed that the university is absolved from all responsibility for the development of students. It is just that a new, viable, realistic formulation must be found which more accurately describes the university-student relationship. Just as it is difficult to hold that the university acts *in loco parentis,* it is equally difficult to maintain that the university-student relationship is one of simple contract since there is an inherent imbalance between the two contracting parties. Seavey maintains that the relationship of the university to its students is that of a fiduciary.

[25] "I have noted elsewhere that there are many practical reasons why *in loco parentis* does not serve as a rationale for university authority in modern times. How does it apply to married students? to part-time students? to students who are totally self-supporting? and especially to students whose parents explicitly state that they want their children 'to be able to make their own decisions when they go to college'?" ("Non-Religious Activities and Spiritual Development," *Christian Wisdom and Christian Formation* [McGannon, Cooke, Klubertanz, eds.], New York: Sheed and Ward, 1964, pp. 256-259.)

A fiduciary is one whose function it is to act for the benefit
of another as to *matters relevant to the relation between them.*
Since schools exist primarily for the education of their students,
it is obvious that professors and administrators act in a fiduciary
capacity with reference to students.[26]

Perhaps, therefore, the university-student relationship is best
understood as that established by a fiduciary contract in
which the "relevant matters" are specified by the stated
educational mission of the university. A fiduciary contract
of this nature would necessarily entail a "limitation of
authority [on the part of the university] to that required
for the genuine needs of the school by its institutional
responsibilities to its students." [27] This inherent limitation
of university authority forestalls criticism that the fiduciary
concept of the university-student relationship is merely
in loco parentis in a disguised form.

The university-student relationship understood as fiduciary has a great advantage in that it provides a guideline
to the reasonable consideration of so many questions which
the university must face. What precisely is the mission of a
university *qua* university? What specific "matters" are relevant to its educational mission? What are the limitations
of the authority which the university exercises in the fulfillment of its institutional responsibilities to its students? What
standards are appropriate and necessary to the fulfillment
of this institutional responsibility? These are the questions
which today are basic to student unrest. The questions are
especially pertinent to Catholic campuses. The Catholic
university which properly understands its mission *qua* university, which limits its concern to matters which are relevant to its educational mission, and which limits the
exercise of its authority to that which is necessary and
appropriate to fulfill its specific institutional responsibilities

[26] Seavey, *op. cit.,* p. 1407. Emphasis added.
[27] Comment, 72 *Yale Law Journal,* p. 1380.

to its students, cannot be accused of either paternalism or
authoritarianism.[28]

[28] Several interesting observations should be added to this consideration of the demise of the *in loco parentis* concept of university authority. Hospitals will probably continue to insist, in an
emergency when parents are unavailable, that a university official
approve any medical procedures which ordinarily require parental
permission. Civil liberty societies will probably continue to insist
that "college authorities should take every practical step to assure
themselves that such students [as have run into police difficulties
off campus in connection with what they regard as their political
rights] are protected in their legal rights" (American Civil Liberties
Union, "Academic Freedom and Civil Liberties of Students in
Colleges and Universities," Revised ed., Nov., 1963). That a university should be asked to perform such functions is difficult to
understand if the university is not acting *in loco parentis* or at
least in some fiduciary capacity. One particular university practice
which strangely enough seems to be becoming increasingly common in public as well as private schools, is especially curious in
this regard. Colleges and universities are having more and more
recourse to parental approval for various student prerogatives particularly with reference to coeds. It is not uncommon, for instance,
for schools to allow coeds (particularly upperclassmen) to live in
apartments off campus or to absent themselves from residence
halls overnight or even over weekends without explanation to
university authorities, *provided that* parents have given their approval. The point at issue is that the university refuses such permissiveness to coeds whose parents do not approve. Is not the
university, in refusing this particular permissiveness to some students, acting *in loco parentis* with respect to those coeds who are
restricted to residence halls and dormitory hours according to the
wishes of their parents? Since the university allows the permissiveness to other coeds it would be difficult to argue, with respect
to those restricted, that the university is enforcing standards which
it judges "appropriate and necessary" to the university community.
Another possible explanation, if *in loco parentis* is denied, is that
the university asks parents, rather than attempts itself, to judge
the "maturity level" of its individual students. The university im-
plicitly enunciates the policy that certain restrictions are necessary
and appropriate only for "immature" students in this particular university community. It then asks the parents to assist in judging
"immaturity." Basing its decision on parental judgment, the university then places restraints on "immature students," not *in loco
parentis,* but on its own authority in fulfillment of its own fiducial

C. "WE WILL MAKE THE RULES"

The third mold that must be broken on the Catholic university campus concerns "substantive" student affairs, the determination of policies, standards and rules especially in the non-academic area. For centuries on Catholic campuses it has been taken for granted, following an accepted clerical tradition, that the administration alone has the right and responsibility to determine these matters. The position is now challenged, and rightly so.

Very little has been said by the courts with respect to "substantive" as opposed to "procedural" problems on university campuses. As long as *in loco parentis* was upheld by the courts, there was no questioning the administration's right to make "any rules or regulations for the government or betterment of their pupils that a parent could make for the same purpose." [29] Even the 1967 Goldberg decision appears to reinforce this position:

The Regents have the general rule-making or policy-making power in regard to the University and are (with exceptions not material here) fully empowered with respect to the organization and government of the University, including the authority to maintain order and decorum on the campus and the

responsibility. The argument seems strained. It provides a curious and interesting inconsistency with respect to developments on present-day campuses. The inconsistency can be solved, of course, by dispensing with all residence-hall requirements for all coeds. After all, the students argue, since there are no restrictions for men living in residence halls on these same campuses, to impose restrictions on women is an obvious case of discrimination—and what university dares be guilty of discrimination in any form in this day and age?

[29] Gott v. Berea College, 156 Ky. 376, 379, 161 S.W. 204, 206 (1913).

enforcement of the same by all appropriate means, including suspension or dismissal from the University.[30]

However, later statements in the Goldberg ruling explain that the power of the Regents is not unlimited. First, constitutional rights may not be needlessly and unreasonably restricted except as required by the very nature of the educational process (Goldberg § 9).[31] Second, the power of the university is limited to making rules which are "appropriate and necessary to the maintenance of order and propriety" in the university community and "reasonably necessary to further the university's educational goals" (§ 15).[32] Finally, the Goldberg opinion refers to the "minimum standards" of propriety in conduct which universities must impose to insure their proper functioning (§ 18). In summary, the Goldberg case appears to establish the position that the power of the university with respect to student conduct is limited to determining "minimum standards" which it considers "necessary and appropriate" to assure "order and propriety" and "to further the university's edu-

[30] Goldberg v. Calif. (36), 1967, p. 468. N.B.: Sections in the Goldberg opinion are numbered. Parenthetical numbers in the following text and footnotes refer to sections in the Goldberg opinion.

[31] For instance, "reasonable restrictions on the [constitutional] freedoms of speech and assembly" may be imposed in view of the university's "valid interest in maintaining good order and decorum" (§ 12). Likewise, "conduct even though intertwined with [the constitutional freedoms of] expression and association is subject to regulation" by the university (§ 13).

[32] It is interesting to note the observation of the court that "in an academic community, greater restrictions may prevail than in society at large" (§ 17). "The subtle fixings of [the] limits [of student freedom] should, in large measure, be left to the educational institution itself" (§ 17). "The University, as an academic community, can formulate its own standards, rewards and punishments to achieve its educational objectives" (§ 27). These latter observations may prove of particular interest in time to private education. (Goldberg v. Calif., 1967.)

cational goals." This would seem to be "freedom where possible and restraint only where necessary" as applied to the unique educational circumstance of the academic community.

What federal and state courts hold with respect to substantive matters in student affairs (policies, standards and rules) is interesting but probably of secondary importance, except where constitutional rights are involved. There is a long-standing tradition in Western society that public as well as private universities should be free to make their own determinations regarding what is "necessary and appropriate" to attain their stated educational goals. It is reasonable to assume that the courts will respect and protect this right of autonomous self-determination even where the nature of the educational enterprise requires a "reasonable" curtailment of constitutional rights. What the courts will consider to constitute "reasonable" where an infringement of constitutional rights is involved may be expected to vary widely from campus to campus depending on the nature of the respective institutions (public or private) and their expressed educational objectives.[33]

[33] A case currently under court consideration is very interesting in this regard. (Gary Dickey v. Alabama State Board of Ed. Decided in favor of Dickey in U.S. District Court, September 8, 1967. Appealed by Alabama Board of Ed. to U.S. District Court of Appeals.)

On August 11, 1967, Dickey was notified by the (Alabama) Troy State College Dean of Men's Office that the Student Affairs Committee "had voted not to (re-)admit him 'at this time.'" This amounted to dismissal, since Dickey had been a student in good standing through the preceding academic year. Since procedural due process had not been observed, Dickey filed a complaint in the District Court. A Student Affairs Committee meeting was subsequently held on August 25, full procedural process being observed. On August 28 Dickey was informed that the Student Affairs Committee had voted to suspend him for one academic year. Dickey then moved through the federal courts for a preliminary injunction "on the theory that his *substantive* rights of due process had been and were being deprived."

Within these limits universities themselves will probably be allowed to determine what is "necessary and appropriate" to attain their own self-determined educational goals. The

---

During the academic year 1967-1968, Dickey, a member of a national honorary journalism fraternity, had served as an editor of the *Tropolitan* (school paper), editor-in-chief of the school literary magazine, copy editor of the yearbook, and editor-in-chief of the student handbook. In April, 1967, he desired to run an editorial in the school paper criticizing the Governor and State Legislature for their stand in an incident which occurred on the University of Alabama campus. Both the faculty advisor to the *Tropolitan* and the President (Adams) of Troy State College forbade Dickey to run the editorial. The advisor provided substitute editorial material entitled "Raising Dogs in North Carolina." Dickey ran only the headline of the originally planned editorial, leaving the rest of the space blank, except for the word "Censored" diagonally across the open space.

The (President) "Adams Rule" was invoked in Dickey's suspension. According to the "Adams Rule," editorials and articles critical of the Governor or State Legislature could not be published in the school paper since "a newspaper could not criticize its owners."

One's first reaction to the circumstances of the Dickey case cannot but be, "You must be kidding." The hypothesis might be advanced that Dickey, the faculty advisor, the Dean of Men, and President Adams contrived in a ridiculous set of circumstances to entice the Governor (Lurleen Wallace) and the State Board of Education into an impossible defense. Dickey's initial dismissal without procedural due process was the first effort to save him. The "Adams Rule" can be construed as a "straw man," which would be taken seriously only in Alabama, and not even there in the federal courts. The substitute editorial contributes to the absurdity. It is an interesting speculation.

The U.S. District has ruled that the "Adams Rule" is not only unnecessary "to maintain order and discipline among the students" on the Troy State College campus but constitutes an unnecessary restriction of the constitutional rights guaranteed by the first and fourteenth amendments. "Regulations and rules which are necessary in maintaining order and discipline are always considered reasonable. [However,] boards of education, presidents of colleges, and faculty advisors are not exempted from the rule that protects students from unreasonable rules and regulations . . . . State school

courts are more liable to reflect the thinking of academe in these matters than to determine it.[34]

On Catholic campuses the power of administration to determine substantive student issues (and procedural matters as well) was held unchallenged for centuries. Student unrest, running the gamut of expression from mere griping to riot, was frequently enough of a factor to be dealt with. However, in all cases administration felt justified in making decisions and taking necessary action unilaterally. Faculty was not a power to be considered since faculty on Catholic campuses was by and large made up of religious who accepted the leadership of the clerical administration as a part of their religious orientation. On Catholic campuses, therefore, administration alone decided what was "necessary and appropriate to the maintenance of order and propriety" and what was "reasonably necessary to further

---

officials cannot infringe on their students' right of free and unrestricted expression as guaranteed by the Constitution . . . where the exercise of such right does not 'materially and substantially interfere with the requirements of appropriate discipline in the operation of the school' (Burnside v. Byars, 363 F 2nd 744, 1966). [Dickey was exercising] his constitutionally guaranteed right of academic and/or political expression."

"There was no legal obligation on the school authorities to permit Dickey to continue as one of [the school newspaper] editors. As a matter of fact, there was no legal obligation on the school authorities to operate a school newspaper. . . . The imposition of such a restraint . . . [as was imposed upon Dickey in this case] violates the basic principles of academic and political expression as guaranteed by our Constitution. . . . 'The essentiality of freedom in the community of American universities is almost self-evident' (Sweezy v. New Hampshire, 354 U.S. 234, 250, 1957)."

[34] In the Dixon opinion Judge Rives cites no academic authorities. However, in the Goldberg case Judge J. Taylor expresses his indebtedness "for help in our analysis" to "many thoughtful comments" which, albeit appearing in legal journals, strongly reflect the thinking more of academe than of legal precedent (§§ 5, 6, footnote).

the university's educational goals." But once again, so much of this has changed. Lay faculty, now significantly outnumbering religious faculty members on most Catholic campuses, demand a voice in university affairs. They no longer consider themselves as employed to teach at a university belonging to some religious community, but rather as partners in an educational enterprise to which they are making an important contribution and in which they are making a considerable personal investment. The extreme faculty position, adapted from the secular educational tradition, is that faculty, not administration, should play the determining role in student affairs since education is basically a faculty-student relationship.

With the emergence of the student concepts of the "right to learn" and responsibility for self-determination, accompanied by a mistrust of "anybody over thirty," students are claiming an increasingly decisive role in all student (academic as well as non-academic) affairs. They must, they assert, bear the final responsibility to prepare themselves for meaningful participation in the social (and educational) revolution which is already occurring in the world about them. The extreme student position is that they can trust only themselves to determine what is truly relevant and meaningful to their own welfare and the future of "their" evolving world. Perceiving administration as the immediate oppressor in the educational situation, student extremists even on Catholic campuses sometimes urge that their own student sector, necessarily autonomous in the university society, must unite with faculty to overthrow the unjust repressions of administrators. Alone or with faculty support, student power must be autonomous and must prevail. Their cause, student leaders feel, is just.

"If you don't give us what we want, we'll have half the people here on the streets within 24 hours. We'll demonstrate, we'll throw up picket lines, we'll block all deliveries. We'll bring this place to a grinding halt." The familiar manifesto has become 1967's favorite litany, emanating from black-power activists, cops and firemen—even teachers.

This time the threat comes from college students. And not just a handful of wishful radicals, either, but well-groomed, articulate undergraduate leaders of 334 U.S. colleges meeting at College Park, Maryland for the National Student Association's annual congress.

They came back to their respective campuses ready to challenge teachers, deans and the whole system of higher education in the U.S. with the rallying cry, "Student power." [35]

A form of university government must emerge on university campuses which provides for "meaningful" and "significant" participation by all sectors of the university community. The legitimate claims of both faculty and students in this regard cannot be dismissed either by trustees or by their appointed university officers. Faculty is making an investment in the university enterprise which can only be adequately recognized and encouraged by their being given a proportionately important role to play in the university's decision-making processes. Students *do* have a responsibility for their own self-development which can be achieved only by their being actively involved in the total university mission. It is, moreover, a bit inconsistent for a university to expect students to assume very serious personal and social responsibilities in the larger society immediately after graduation but to allow them no opportunity to assume personal and community responsibilities in the university society as undergraduates.

All sectors of the university must participate in the determination of university affairs. But what shall the mixture be? And who will determine precisely how much voice the administration, faculty and student sectors should have in

[35] "Now it's Student Power," *Life* (Special Report), October 27, 1967, p. 91. Reprinted by permission.

various decisions? There is no easy answer to these questions since circumstances will vary so much from campus to campus. If, however, the emphasis in university government were less on preserving traditional decision-making prerogatives and more on educating and encouraging others to assume policy determining responsibilities, there would be fewer tensions in most Catholic universities. The unique insights of students into their own needs cannot be overlooked as a qualification for participation in university government. Student participation should be encouraged not as play-acting, or as an educational experience, or, worst of all, as a concession to student power. It should be respected because students through their insights have something unique and very significant to contribute to many important areas of university government.

It is by no means to be presumed that all Catholic universities will have identical educational goals for identical student bodies with identical student needs. Neither is it to be presumed, therefore, that the same policies, standards and rules will be uniformly "appropriate and necessary" for all Catholic university campuses. However, granting this diversity, the ideal of a true university will be approached on Catholic campuses insofar as each academic community in its unique circumstance is able to provide policies, standards and rules which encourage free student inquiry and expression.

What should the norm be in the future for decisions which Catholic university communities will make with respect to substantive student issues? The answer can only be: Freedom where possible, restraint only where necessary. With all sectors of the community significantly participating, each Catholic university will have to decide for itself, according to the above general norm, what policies, standards and rules are "reasonably necessary to further the university's educational goals." Where a high degree of student responsibility has already developed it is not in the least unreasonable that the university community should delegate a nearly total authority to the student sector in determining matters which pertain almost exclusively to the student interest. To work toward such a high degree of student responsibility should be the goal of every university community.

But will not abuses occur if students are allowed such freedom in the Catholic academic community? The only honest answer is: Yes, student abuses of freedom will definitely occur. It must reasonably be anticipated that where students are encouraged to express themselves openly and vocally they will from time to time express themselves irresponsibly. Perhaps particularly on Catholic campuses abuses of freedom of expression should be expected since there is no long tradition of freedom in Catholic pre-college education. It can be expected, for instance, that Catholic university students will at times use the opportunity provided by censorless publications to express a strong reaction to authoritarian and paternalistic, and perhaps puritanical, aspects of their past family, parish and high-school experience. Precisely because of their protected backgrounds, Catholic university students may manifest a singular imprudence when first allowed a true freedom of expression. And it may well happen that student abuses of freedom in a particular circumstance may be such that it will be "appropriate and necessary" for the university community, all sectors participating in the decision, temporarily to restrict certain freedoms in view of a particular university's educational goals. However, this should be seen as an unfortunate and temporary situation.

The freedom which the academic community can with confidence allow students should always be regarded as a measure of educational achievement. One of the purposes of the academic enterprise is to educate students to a responsible use of freedom. Policies, standards and rules should frequently be adjusted by the university community to take into account the capacity of each student generation (the character of which changes almost every year) to assume freedom with responsibility.

D. THE PASSIVE STUDENT

The fourth mold to be broken on the Catholic university campus, if student affairs are to meet the standards of a true university, concerns the part students should play in their own education. Until recent times students on Catholic campuses were expected not so much to learn as to be taught. As has already been noted, "the whole thrust of the old system was in the direction of inculcating in students a previously arrived at synthesis of secular knowledge, intellectual skills, ethical values and religious truths." [36] If students in Catholic universities were not explicitly taught, they soon enough came to believe, that the Church had all the answers, at least all the answers that really mattered. Accordingly, if students just absorbed what the Catholic university had to teach, their proper education was assured. There was no need for students to be concerned about or involved in planning their own educational development.

Great changes have come about. Having all the answers was but one aspect of the triumphalism which the Church repudiated at the Second Vatican Council. Long before the Council, however, it was apparent to many Catholic educators that the all-answer syndrome of Catholic education served only to isolate Catholic universities from the many valuable mainstreams of thought in academe. The growth of Catholic graduate schools, which cannot be isolated, the influx of lay faculty from non-Catholic institutions, the

[36] Gleason, "Crisis in Catholic Universities," p. 51.

professionalization of Catholic universities' faculties—all these have helped to break down the isolation of Catholic universities and have served to integrate thought on Catholic campuses with that of the larger academic community. Not the least factor in this breakdown of Catholic educational isolationalism was the agitation of students on Catholic campuses to assert their "right to learn."

The student "right to learn," like academic freedom, can become an all-purpose shibboleth. Basically, however, it involves two very important principles, the right of free inquiry and the right of free expression. Both are essential if students are to be allowed to play a realistically free, self-determining role in their own education. Students must be free to inquire wherever they feel any element of truth might be found. They must also be free to express their present convictions, since campus dialogue is a genuine means for seeking truth and clarifying convictions. The right to organize and join student organizations for the freer and more forceful expression of ideas, the right to invite outside speakers to campus to challenge or reinforce academic positions, and the right to express views openly in student publications are all corollaries to the rights of free inquiry and free expression. These rights are based on academic needs, needs which must be fulfilled by students who are sincere in the pursuit of truth as the basis of their own self-formation.

Students today are impatient with and suspicious of any efforts to protect them from ideas which their elders deem harmful to young minds. And perhaps understandably so. They abhor any ban on speakers and distrust whoever would impose such a ban. "Will he tell us something you don't want us to know?" they ask. "Are you afraid for us, or really for yourselves?" Editors of student publications want to know why their ideas are regarded as an impertinence if they disagree with some cherished institutional value. "Is the system more vulnerable than we suspected?" they wonder. Whatever the merits of such instruments as the Index of Forbidden Books in bygone years, the idea is anathema today. Students suspect it was anathema from its inception and regard with deep mistrust a system of education, and those responsible for the system, which used such means to achieve educational goals. They cannot but notice that the thought of Martin Luther is today being very carefully studied by Catholic scholars and is now acknowledged to merit deep consideration by Catholic students. Yet just a generation ago Martin Luther was hurriedly dismissed on the Catholic university campus as an "adversary" along with a brief summary of his "errors." Students know today that a great deal of truth is to be found where their fathers were forbidden to search. Is there any wonder that the present student reaction of mistrust is sometimes extended to "everybody over thirty"? Total freedom appears to students to be the only ideal which can currently be reconciled with their need to inquire and express their views in the academic society.

The problems of Catholic universities in recognizing the students' "right to learn" are not easily resolved after centuries of self-isolation. There are some very important responsibilities which Catholic universities feel obliged to fulfill; these responsibilities appear to run counter to the "right to learn" as it is frequently interpreted. The most basic responsibility which the Catholic university feels obliged to fulfill is that of instruction in the areas of philosophy and theology. Any instruction in these areas on the collegiate level appears inappropriate to some as jeopardizing if not completely frustrating the student "right to learn." For instance, Frederick Crosson feels that there is no place in the Catholic university for religious instruction:

The primary function of the university is not instruction but inquiry. . . . For example theology . . . in college ought not to be doctrinal instruction but reflective theorizing. Further instruction may indeed be necessary if "literacy" is lacking, and in the case of the sciences especially it may be that the language skill necessary to read "the great book of nature" will not be mastered before graduate school. But this cannot be the excuse for an indefinite delay of critical inquiry if the student has sufficient command of the "language" to formulate meaningful questions in the area.[37]

On what basis Crosson judges that students entering college can be presumed to be theologically "literate" and already possessed of "the language skill" necessary to read God's greatest book is not explained. In American universities, instruction on the undergraduate level is as necessary in the "science" of theology as in the other sciences if the study is to be truly meaningful and productive. Yet, Crosson's position merits serious consideration. If the students' "right to learn" is to be taken seriously on Catholic campuses, even during the early undergraduate years, doctrinal instruction cannot be offered as the sole fare. Freshmen and sophomores do have sufficient command of the "language" to face *some* critical questions in theology. Moreover, with respect to these questions, students have a right, not just to the answers proffered by Catholic teaching, but to an honest and understanding presentation of all answers which are seriously proposed today by men of thought. In other words, university students have a right to see the Catholic answers in full historical and critical context. All of this should be part of university instruction.

If the Catholic university has a responsibility for the theological instruction of its undergraduates it seems a bit

[37] Crosson, Frederick, "Personal Commitment as the Basis of Free Inquiry," *Academic Freedom And The Catholic University* (Manier and Houck, eds.), Notre Dame, Indiana: Fides Publishers, Inc., 1967, pp. 89-90.

difficult to argue that the Catholic university represents the "Church learning," but not the "Church teaching." At least with respect to undergraduates the Catholic university must be something of both. In providing instruction for undergraduates it is obviously performing a teaching function. Just how the teaching function of the Catholic university is to be disassociated from the teaching function of the Church, as Rev. John Walsh proposes, is not clear.

It is a very serious mistake to speak of the Catholic university as a part of the teaching function of the Roman Catholic Church or even its teaching apostolate.
To think of the Catholic university as an instrument of the Church for the carrying out of its teaching mission leads, I think, both to serious misunderstanding of the Church's teaching mission in itself and to profound distortions of the nature of a university.[38]

The urge to assert autonomy for the Catholic university, undoubtedly essential in certain areas of university life, cannot be so easily extended to the instructional function of the Catholic university. A Catholic university cannot with honesty teach its own brand of Catholicism. There is only one Catholicism and this is what is passed on by the magisterium of the Church. It is almost overstating the obvious to say that students at a Catholic university have a "right to learn" the official teaching of the Catholic magisterium. The Catholic university, therefore (and not just the local ordinary), has a corresponding responsibility to see that the authentic teaching of the magisterium is adequately presented on the Catholic university campus.

The fulfillment of this instructional responsibility in no way repudiates the dignity and even autonomy of theology as a science in the Catholic university setting. Quite the contrary: religious instruction appropriately conceived for

[38] Walsh, John E., "The University And The Church," *Academic Freedom And The Catholic University*, p. 108.

the university situation will supplement the higher approach to theology as a science. Walsh's point is well made if Catholic university instruction is *necessarily* limited to teaching exclusively a "given set of doctrines, values, or attitudes . . . ; the teachings of the Church." But Catholic instruction on the university level is not *per se* so limited. As has already been pointed out, Catholic universities have a serious responsibility to present the teachings of the magisterium in a full historical and critical context. In so doing, however, the Catholic university is not disassociating itself from the "Church teaching," but rather adapting its instruction to the educational needs and "right to learn" of university students.

What is the responsibility of the Catholic university "to guide" students and how can guidance be reconciled with the students' personal responsibility of self-determination? Is not any effort to guide students bound to prejudice the presentation, predetermine the answer, and consequently destroy the students' independent "right to learn"? The true Catholic university, John Cogley seems to assert, not only has *no* responsibility to guide its students, but as a university has a responsibility precisely *not* to guide students. Its primary responsibility, Cogley holds, is to open up to students all possible avenues of speculation and choice.

I think that today every university has a duty to teach its students what Freud had to say, *precisely as Freud wanted to be understood*. It also has the duty to teach its students what Freud's critics had to say, precisely as *they* wanted to be understood. The same goes for Marx, Nietzsche, for Hume, Spengler, Wittgenstein, Bertrand Russell, as well as for St. Thomas, Niebuhr and Sartre. I do not believe that any university, precisely because it is a university, can play favorites among these giants. I do not believe that any university should indoctrinate its students in the teachings of any of them. By the same token, every university is bound to expose its students

to the thought of all of them and be committed institutionally
to none.[39]

In Cogley's view "universities cannot play favorites." His
further comments are extremely relevant to a clear understanding of his argument.

This demand can be made on all universities precisely because
they are universities. I do not believe that today *any* university can be uncritically committed as an institution to a
particular philosophy, political system, to any one religion or
anti-religion. By the same token, the university can not exclude
from thoughtful consideration any ideology, philosophy, political system or religion which living men of learning, by common agreement, deem worthy of consideration.

Obviously, this means theology belongs in every university—
whether it is called Catholic, Protestant, or secular. In a certain
sense, then, a "secular" university is as anomalous a term as
"Catholic" university.

As Miss Stein might have put it, a university is a university
is a university.[40]

Cogley's argument is honest.[41] The world and our nation
have need of such universities as Cogley describes. Since
"some great minds have addressed themselves to the ultimate questions that are put under the heading of theology,"
it might well be argued that public universities have a re-

---

[39] Cogley, John, "The Future Of An Illusion," *Commonweal*,
June 2, 1967, p. 313.

[40] *Ibid.,* p. 313-314.

[41] Cogley proposes and answers what he feels to be the most
serious objection to his concept of the true (Catholic) university.
"Then, one must ask: Can the university-as-such 'believe in God'?"
Are those who do not, or have ceased to, believe excluded from
the university community? Moreover, should the university-as-such
"reflect that belief in every aspect of its operation"? Here, I realize,
is a difficult problem. But if one replies yes, what happens to
agnosticism and atheism on such campuses? Should they be out-
lawed as unworthy of consideration?—are they to be triumphantly
confuted?—is the argument settled before it begins?

sponsibility to provide "genuinely pluralistic" departments of philosophy and theology,[42] not just courses in the history of these disciplines. Professional learned and civil liberty societies might well address themselves to seeing that the student "right to learn" is fulfilled in this regard on public campuses. And if the present interpretation of our national constitution precludes such a possibility (to the extreme detriment of public education, it would appear), perhaps some private schools should address themselves to the fulfillment of this obvious public need.

However, it is only reasonable to point out that in order to achieve Cogley's ideal, which requires that the university play no favorites with particular philosophies and theologies, it would appear necessary that the campus atmosphere be neither religious nor areligious. What is perhaps more to the point, any guidance of students beyond

---

St. Thomas Aquinas begins the *Summa* with the question *an Deus sit?* and takes the question seriously. If a university seriously asks its students the same question (and every university should), can it then carry on as if the question is not a real one, with only one answer intellectually tolerable? "The fool has said in his heart there is no God" is a Biblical judgment. But like Saint Thomas, the university can not carry on as if all who question God's existence are patently foolish and unworthy of consideration: even the Scriptures are not self-evident.

[42] The charge of indoctrination is so frequently raised in criticism of Catholic education. I have noted elsewhere that, "To fulfill its purpose and achieve its mission, the university must be allowed, even by the State and Church which authorizes its existence, a great deal of independence and freedom. The State cannot use the public university to mold jingoistic patriots, nor can the Church use Catholic universities to form "pious, passive believers," without completely frustrating the main educational mission of the university itself. The university neither fulfills its own purpose nor best serves the State and Church if it allows its mission to be subverted to immediate and shortsighted needs of the State and Church" ("Student Rights and Freedoms on the Catholic University Campus—Background Considerations and Norms," *National Catholic Educational Association Bulletin*, August, 1966, p. 229).

an advanced instruction in how to read and how to study, however well intentioned, would destroy the neutrality which is essential to this type of university. If the student choice is to be absolutely free, personal influence of every kind both inside and outside the classroom would have to be carefully avoided. It is only fair to ask, is such a university possible? Would only this type of campus really provide the necessary circumstances for a truly effective search for truth? Is such a campus necessary, or ideal, to fulfill the student "right to learn"?

In the present existential circumstance, at least, it would seem that Catholic universities can play another more productive role in higher education. This is not totally to disregard the Cogley ideal. It is only to say that at the present time it is more realistic to regard the total academe as the universal university Cogley envisions and to say that within this total academe the Catholic university has a unique service to perform.

The Cogley concept of the ideal (Catholic) university fails to consider, it would appear, the nature and importance of religious faith in a student's life. If it is presumed that the choice of ultimate beliefs is purely a rational choice, Cogley's university would unquestionably be the only true ideal. If the minds of students upon entering a university were *tabula rasa,* or even if in an ideal order it were best that upon entering the university the minds of students were as *"rasa"* as possible, again Cogley's university would be the ideal. But it is neither a fact that the minds of students are *tabula rasa* when they enter the university nor is it an ideal that they should be. The important factor of religious faith must be taken into consideration.

Students entering a university are already persons; this is saying a great deal. The most important aspect of their personhood is that through seventeen or so years they

have encountered God's own Self in their every free decision. In a different measure for each freshman God has
elicited from each of them a trust and faith. In different
measure and in different ways they believe in God—and
this is the most important thing about individual freshmen.
With respect to ultimate values and ultimate beliefs, with
respect to God Himself, the minds of students entering the
university are not *tabula rasa,* however much such a religious condition might appear to exist even to individual
freshmen themselves.

Is it so wrong that students of like faith, of like relationship to God, should freely choose to search for truth in an
academic community of men who share their faith? Does
faith itself, or an association with men of like faith, automatically and *per se* preclude the possibility of a free and
unprejudiced search for truth? Might it not be that for
some students the search for truth and the possibility of
self-fulfillment will be positively aided by an association
with men who share the insights which a common religious
faith generates? To provide a milieu for those Catholic
(and non-Catholic) students who conscientiously feel that
they can most freely and effectively seek further truth and
their own personal self-fulfillment in such an association
is the mission of the Catholic university.

To say all this about the mission of the Catholic university is not to say enough. The mission will almost necessarily be misunderstood and misinterpreted unless the
necessary relationship of the Catholic university to the
total academe is clearly perceived. This relationship is one
of both need and service.

Only at its own peril can the Catholic university seek to
fulfill its internal educational function in isolation from
the rest of academe. If the sciences of philosophy and
theology are to be "genuinely" pursued on the Catholic
campus, there must be a constant exchange with philoso-

phers and theologians on other campuses throughout all of academe. There must be an understanding response to suggestions and criticisms from academe to philosophical and theological developments (or the lack thereof) on the Catholic campus. The Catholic university must recognize its dependence for the knowledge it must obtain from academe in allied sciences—anthropology, ethnology, psychology, sociology, comparative religions, etc.—in order to develop the sciences of philosophy and theology on its own campus. In these and many other ways the Catholic university must accept and appreciate its desperate need to function not in isolation but in continual contact with all other colleges and universities.

On the other hand the Catholic university must recognize the unique service it is called upon to provide academe.[43] It is the mission of the Catholic university, and of all private universities that search for new truth with the unique insights which a community commitment provides, to suggest possible new approaches to the problems which confront the larger academic community. Can the students' "right to learn" be properly respected in a Catholic university so conceived? Most definitely, provided that both instruction and guidance direct students to a perception of their religious faith and the insights it provides not only in full historical and critical context but in the perspective of the current pursuit of related truth in the larger academic society. For some students the "right to learn" can

[43] Richardson, William J., "Pay Any Price? Break Any Mold?" *America*, April 29, 1967, p. 625. "In the world of Academia, then, where institutions live together as so many corporate persons, it is altogether fitting that there be institutions among them that incorporate the values of Christianity in general and of Catholicism in particular. In a word, the role of a Catholic university today is to represent the Church in Academia, i.e., to serve as that corporate person through which the Church becomes present to the community of academic institutions and they to it."

only be adequately provided in such an educational milieu. These students will undoubtedly pursue new truth most effectively and achieve their greatest self-fulfillment in a Catholic university community which is

dedicated to a courageous, unrelenting and radical reflection on the cosmic meaning of Christendom's dedication to Christ.[44]

———

The fifth "mold to be broken" on the Catholic university campus, that which pertains to the religious development of students, will be considered in the next chapter.

[44] Crosson, "Personal Commitment," p. 90.

IV

*Student Religious Development**

A. STUDENT RESPONSIBILITY FOR SELF-DEVELOPMENT

IN THE PREVIOUS CHAPTER four "molds to be broken" were discussed with relation to the Catholic university's achieving "its true function as a university." In this article a fifth such mold will be considered. If the Catholic university is to achieve its true function, some long-cherished concepts of religious development will have to be abandoned as the whole religious program is reoriented to the evolving mission of the Catholic university in academe. This is not to say that the religious development of students will become less important to the Catholic university. Quite the contrary: in proportion to the Catholic university's striving to fulfill its unique mission in academe

* March, 1968; revised.

the centrality of student religious development on Catholic campuses will become more and more apparent. It is not the necessity of student religious development which will be discussed in this chapter but the nature and manner of its accomplishment.

It has already been noted that most sectarian institutions of higher learning, Protestant as well as Catholic, were established with the religious formation of youth as their primary goal. The statement of the Civil War president of Amherst College would be typical for most Protestant (and Catholic) colleges of the era.

What is the province of the college? It is by instruction, discipline, and all good influence to make *men,* especially Christian men, and most of all ministers of Christ, and those of the highest order of character. . . . I would have the college for all coming time the most powerful engine for building up the Kingdom of our Redeemer.[1]

It probably never entered the mind of any Amherst president of the nineteenth century that the primary purpose of the college could be anything else than the Christian formation of youth. It was presumed that Amherst adequately possessed all the truth that was essential to the proper formation of Christian men, "and most of all ministers of Christ." The formation of Christian men, therefore, not the pursuit of new truth, was the primary goal of almost all early sectarian education in our country.

Catholic colleges in the United States were not established, as were so many Protestant colleges, for the specific purpose of training the clergy. In the sixteenth century the Council of Trent had specified that the Catholic clergy should be formed in houses of study which would be isolated from all lay influence. While it might reasonably have been expected that a good Catholic college would

[1] Quoted by Michael P. Walsh, *op. cit.,* p. 46.

produce its measure of young men who would freely choose later to enter the Catholic seminary, the purpose of the Catholic college itself was to form Catholic lay students for a future life as laymen in the "secular city."

By no means, however, was the Catholic college free from seminary influence. Isolation from the secular world, advocated for Catholic seminaries, was considered equally appropriate for Catholic colleges. Many Catholic colleges were established in what at that time were places remote, and safe, from the everyday world. By and large it was presumed that the techniques of religious formation proper to the seminary of that time were, with accommodations, appropriate to the religious formation of lay students on the Catholic campus. Courses in theology and philosophy were usually simplified versions of those offered in the seminary. Co-curricular religious formation programs also followed the pattern of seminary training. Specified religious exercises were required, and accepted, as a necessary means of religious formation.

It is not at all strange that until recent times many Catholic colleges were established in remote areas and characterized by a seminary-type education. Most Catholic colleges were, after all, founded by members of religious orders or congregations familiar with no other manner of education. Moreover, the advisability of isolating sectarian schools from irreligious and secular influences was characteristic of all religious thinking of the day. Then too, during the nineteenth century almost all Catholic colleges offered only a six-year combined high school–college program to an unsophisticated student group ranging from thirteen to eighteen years of age. Curricula were limited and fairly rigid. External discipline was strictly enforced, although this point has perhaps been exaggerated. In such small schools faculty-student contacts were necessarily close and personal. The authoritarianism and paternalism which unquestionably characterized Catholic education of this period was balanced in large part by deep personal concern and thoughtful benevolence. So many alumni of these schools strongly attest that there existed on these small Catholic college campuses a great deal of faculty-student understanding, respect and love.

Catholic educators of this early American period saw little value in contacts with the secular academe which was considered (and not without reason) to be dominated by either irreligious or anti-Catholic forces. On Catholic campuses young students could be protected, as it was thought proper to protect them, from the influence of ideas which were at least alien if not openly hostile to Catholic thought and practice. On such campuses young boys could be taught Christian truth and formed in Christian character with little interference from external, disturbing influences. In the educational tradition of the time, students were expected to play an almost passive role in their religious development. Theological speculation was not considered a function of these early Catholic colleges. The college perceived itself primarily as a *communicator*. It communicated "the teaching of the Church" which had been formulated by theologians, canon lawyers, and a hierarchy quite removed from the Catholic campus. Religious character was developed by teaching students to conform to predetermined patterns of Christian social behavior. In so conforming, students developed essential habits of Christian character.

It is easy to oversimplify, and in so doing to caricature and thereby to grossly misrepresent Catholic college education of this earlier period. With hindsight, that education can undoubtedly be faulted. It is apparent today that the Catholic college program of the nineteenth and early twentieth centuries did not adequately prepare graduates for the revolutionary social, political, and religious changes the world is currently experiencing. Quite the contrary: sharing the blindness of social injustice which character- ized all education of the era, Catholic colleges in their own way helped to strengthen a now unacceptable *status quo*. Nevertheless there was absolutely no intellectual hypocrisy or dishonesty in early Catholic college education. At that time and in those circumstances it was thought that the Catholic college, so conceived and so conducted, presented to students all the religious and secular truths necessary for their becoming responsible parents and active members of society. The program of religious formation was strongly allied to disciplines in the humanities which possibly taught students more truth about themselves and their fellow men than many of the "relevant" courses of our own day. While Catholic students in these earlier colleges might not have seen their faith in full critical context, they probably per- ceived its inner congruity and its meaning for their per- sonal lives more clearly than do most students today. The intimate faculty-student association in these schools devel- oped an idealism in their lives which fulfilled many of the current demands for personalism in education.

The religious formation programs of the day stressed the illumination provided by religious faith, the personal rela- tionship of the individual to God, and the function of the Church not just to provide a means of union with Christ but especially to teach, guide, and unify its members. Admittedly, the manner of imparting this illumination was largely catechetical, and religious formation was character- ized in large part by external regulation. Such techniques were considered appropriate to education at that time. In retrospect, it must be conceded that the programs were largely successful. Judging by the circumstances, by pre- vailing social attitudes, and particularly by the limited goals that were sought, there is no reason to fault the religious development programs of early American Catholic

colleges. These colleges *did* successfully prepare generations of responsible Catholic parents and citizens according to the needs and standards of the times.

Now, however, there is reason to believe that what might
have constituted reasonably successful religious development programs in the previous century are quite inappropriate today. Many things have changed. Just after the turn
of the century, Catholic higher education adopted the
secular pattern which provided that four years of college
work should be completely distinct from the four high
school years. As a result, many changes took place on
Catholic campuses to which religious development programs have been adjusted only gradually. The age of college students was automatically raised by almost four years.
As the colleges grew, the intimate, personal character of
many campuses was lost. The liberal arts character of
Catholic education suffered considerably as curricula were
expanded to satisfy pre-professional and secular vocational
demands. After the Second World War, many Catholic
colleges began offering graduate programs. Older and more
sophisticated students, well informed of student developments on secular campuses, demanded in Catholic universities a greater freedom of inquiry and expression as essential
to their new academic status.

The most significant development with respect to religious formation on Catholic campuses was the gradual
evolution of the concept that students should be encouraged
to play a more mature, self-determining role in their own
educational development. It was inevitable that a parallel
concept should evolve—that students should be encouraged
to play a more mature, self-determining role in their religious formation. Reinforcing this new student role are the
many statements of Pope John XXIII and the Second
Vatican Council insisting that educators develop in stu-

dents a strong sense of personal responsibility for everything that affects their lives, both secular and religious.

As increased personal responsibility has been placed on
university students for their own self-development, religious
as well as academic, some Catholic educators have advocated that all student religious programs, both curricular
and co-curricular, should be voluntary. They feel, moreover, that this is essential to the Catholic university's functioning as a true university. However, by far the majority
of Catholic educators consider it inadvisable to move
abruptly to completely voluntary religious programs and
that such a change is not necessary for a Catholic university to function as a true university.

On most Catholic campuses, while very serious efforts
are being made to adapt existing religious development
programs to the changing times, the changes in the Church,
the changing mentality of the student body, and the changes
in education itself, very few of these well-intentioned
adaptations have any apparent relation to developing in
students an increasing competence precisely as *students* in
a Catholic university community. As a result, many
campus religious development programs appear to students
to be not only inappropriate but totally irrelevant to their
overall university experience. Changes and adaptations of
older programs, therefore, are not enough. If there has
evolved a new and unique mission for the Catholic university in academe, campus religious development programs
must prepare students to play an increasingly active role
in the university's fulfillment of this mission.

B. "BROADENED AND INTENSIFIED" CAMPUS RELIGIOUS PROGRAMS

A full consideration of religious development programs
for Catholic universities must take into account not only

the role which students must play as members of an academic community but also the responsibilities they will be
expected to fulfill as Catholic laymen in a secular society.
The Second Vatican Council indicates that the lay apostolate must be "thoroughly broadened and intensified." [2] If
the campus religious program is to prepare students for
this particular apostolate it would seem apparent that university religious development programs must be correspondingly broadened and intensified.

The Second Vatican Council indicates quite clearly that
programs intended to prepare students for the broadened
and intensified lay apostolate are not to be merely adaptations of seminary programs. "Since laymen share in their
own way in the mission of the Church, their apostolic
formation [must take] its special flavor from the distinctively secular quality of the lay state and from its own
form of spirituality." The Council provides some general
guidelines for developing this "distinctively secular" form
of lay spirituality. "Doctrinal instruction," for instance, is
to be "adjusted to the age, status and natural talents" of
particular student groups. Students must develop their own
special "sensitivity to the movement of the Holy Spirit."
They must be "well informed in the modern world" and
prepared to serve as "active members in society, adjusted
to its culture." They must respect "truly human values,
especially the art of living fraternally with others." While
most of these qualities would be of advantage to the
clergy, taken together they provide a "special flavor" and a
"distinctive secular quality" for lay spirituality.[3]

Two years before the Council promulgated its decrees on
lay spirituality, Pope John addressed himself to a consideration of lay spiritual formation in the pastoral exhorta-

[2] *Documents, Vatican II*, "Decree on the Apostolate of the Laity"
§ 1 (p. 490).
[3] *Ibid.*, § 29 (pp. 516-517).

tion section of his encyclical letter, *Peace on Earth*. His admonitions cannot be overlooked by those responsible for the spiritual development of students on Catholic campuses.

It is necessary that human beings, in the intimacy of their own consciences, should so live and act in their temporal lives as to create a synthesis between scientific, technical and professional elements on the one hand, and spiritual values on the other.

It is not enough, Pope John points out, that Catholics "be illumined with the gift of faith and enkindled with the desire of forwarding a good cause." They must be prepared "to take an active part in various organizations and influence them from within" with the result that the relationships of society are elevated

to an order that is genuinely human, that is, to an order whose foundation is truth, whose measure and objective is justice, whose driving force is love and whose method of attainment is freedom.[4]

In a consideration of campus religious development programs it is especially important to note Pope John's inclusion of freedom in this particular context. Truth, justice, and love are traditional and obvious values in a Christian society. Pope John, however, adds a fourth value, freedom, giving it equal stature with truth, justice, and love. This is because Pope John, and subsequently the Second Vatican Council, were so concerned with everything relevant to the dignity of the human person. The fullness of man's dignity can be achieved only in a society which has a deep understanding of and respect for not only truth, justice, and love but also freedom. These four elements are proposed as essential to a society which is "genuinely human." Along with concern for the dignity of man, therefore, the four

[4] Pope John XXIII, *Peace on Earth* (New York: The America Press, 1963), §§ 147-150.

basic elements of a "genuinely human" society are especially relevant to campus programs for spiritual development.

Freedom is a matter of such tremendous stress in the modern academic world that its proper understanding must be a particular concern of university religious development programs. It is important, therefore, to note that the Council in its consideration of freedom sees no contradiction between true freedom and the moral obligations which truth imposes.

It is in accordance with their dignity as persons—that is, being endowed with reason and free will and therefore privileged to bear personal responsibility—that all men should be at once impelled by nature and also bound by a moral obligation to seek the truth, especially religious truth. They are also bound to adhere to the truth, once it is known, and to order their whole lives in accord with the demands of truth.[5]

Not without its special significance for campus religious development programs is the Council's definition of man's dignity as a person: "beings . . . privileged to bear personal responsibility." Equally important is the lack of contradiction that the Council finds between true freedom and true obedience.

[Let] everyone, especially those who are charged with the task of educating others, do their utmost to form men who will respect moral order and be obedient to lawful authority. Let them form men too who will be lovers of freedom—men, in other words, who will come to decisions on their own judgment and in the light of truth, govern their activities with a sense of responsibility, and strive after what is true and right, willing always to join with others in cooperative effort.

Religious freedom, therefore, ought to have this further aim,

[5] *Documents, Vatican II,* "Declaration on Religious Freedom" § 2 (p. 679).

namely, that men may come to act with greater responsibility in fulfilling their duties in community life.[6]

It has been said that a full theology of the layman has yet to be written, that Pope John and the Second Vatican Council have only initiated the task. If this is true, programs for spiritual development on Catholic campuses can at this time only reflect the thrust and direction that this theology is currently taking. The following four points indicate what appear to be obvious trends in the "broadening and intensifying" of lay spirituality as it applies to Catholic university programs. *First,* religious development programs for university students must have their own "special flavor." They are not to be mere adaptations of seminary programs reflecting a spirituality appropriate to the clergy. Since it is the peculiar vocation of laymen to work in the "secular city," student spirituality must have its own "distinctive secular quality." *Second,* university religious programs must develop in students a competence "to come to decisions on their own judgment," particularly an ability to coordinate scientific, technical and professional knowledge with religious values. They must, moreover, develop a special "sensitivity to the Holy Spirit" under whose direction they must seek to give direction to evolving temporal affairs. *Third,* human dignity must be a primary concern of student spirituality. Both as members of a university community and as members of a secular society students must work toward a society which is "genuinely human," a society in which truth, justice, love and freedom are increasingly realized; only in such a society will human dignity be fully respected. *Fourth,* students must hold in high esteem the role of service. "The desire of forwarding a good cause" is not enough. Desire must lead in turn to concern, experience in the

[6] *Ibid.,* § 8 (p. 687).

techniques of social change, and ultimately to involved service.

These appear to be the principal features which must be incorporated into broadened and intensified Catholic university religious development programs. Traditional values must obviously be retained—the illumination provided by divine faith, the personal relationship of each individual to God, and the function of the Church—not just as a means of corporate union with Christ but as teacher and guide. The manner of respecting and communicating both traditional and new values, however, must be peculiarly adapted to the university milieu. Broadened and intensified campus religious programs must serve to involve students in the academic mission of the Catholic university community. The development in students of both the traditional and the new "distinctively secular" religious qualities must occur as a precise result of students' participating in a faith-oriented academic community.

C. A TOTAL UNIVERSITY PROJECT

It is difficult to see how the Catholic university can produce laymen possessing the qualities of such a broadened and intensified lay spirituality unless the total university is involved in students' religious formation. For one thing, a university cannot teach values which it does not itself corporately exemplify. A Catholic university cannot communicate a "distinctive secular quality" of spirituality unless the total university life reflects its own distinctive secular quality. Students cannot learn "to come to decisions on their own judgment" and to develop a "sensitivity to the Holy Spirit" unless they are encouraged to make important decisions on the university campus. They cannot be expected to develop a sense of human dignity and a concept of society which is "genuinely human" unless as students they are encouraged to search for truth, seek justice, experience fraternal love, and cherish freedom.

These qualities can be developed only on a campus where the exercise of authority and the correlative obedience are proportioned to the educational and academic objectives of a true university. Catholic students, moreover, will develop a mature sense of service and mission to the larger secular society only in a university which itself projects an image of service and mission within the larger academe. It is not the details of the spiritual development program, therefore, that are of first importance to the Catholic university, but rather the spirit and character of the total university itself. The spirit and character of the total Catholic university, precisely as a Catholic university, must be thoroughly broadened and intensified, completely renewed [7] where necessary, if the university is to communicate to its students the qualities of lay spirituality enunciated by Pope John and the Second Vatican Council.

To understand how the renewed Catholic university is to achieve this goal it is necessary to review some concepts treated earlier. Most important of all, the Catholic university must function as a true university which means that its primary goal must be a search for new truth. Aided by the special insights which religious faith provides, the Catholic university must see itself as providing a unique service within the larger academe. If the Catholic university attempts to exist in isolation this unique mission cannot be

---

[7] The term "renewed" is used in the sense explained by John J. McEleney, S.J., in his introduction to the "Decree on the Appropriate Renewal of the Religious Life." "One of the basic points for consideration of this conciliar Decree consists precisely in the clear distinction between *adaptation* and renewal: the former term is concerned with changes that are necessary on behalf of external contemporary needs and the outward circumstances of our times, whereas the term *renewal* refers to interior renovation of the spirit. . ." (*Documents, Vatican II*, p. 464).

fulfilled. Only by means of a continuous, critical, yet understanding interchange of insights and ideas with secular
academe can the Catholic university hope to achieve its
corporate academic mission, while at the same time providing the conditions which are essential to the religious development of students. In so functioning the Catholic university will manifest the "distinctive secular quality" which
is essential to student spirituality while in no way relin-
quishing its equally distinctive religious character.

And it is of utmost importance, both to its functioning
as a true university and to its fulfilling its unique mission in
the larger academe, that the Catholic university corporately
possess and project a distinctive religious character. At the
renewed Catholic university, therefore, the religious development of students cannot be considered extrinsic or acci-
dental to the university's purpose and function, but rather
as absolutely essential to its *academic* mission within
academe. The religious development of students is essential because religious faith in its most profound expression
is a community virtue. It is not individuals on the Catholic
university campus but the total Catholic university community which must employ its special religious-faith insights to the search for new truth. It is the total Catholic
university community, *students necessarily included,* which,
as a corporate member of academe, must serve academe by
its unique contribution to the general pursuit of new truth.

The basic function of the religious development program
on a Catholic university campus, therefore, must be to incorporate students into an academic community which,
while functioning as a true university, is *alive* and *vibrant*
with its own unique faith and insights. Through the religious development program students must be brought
freely to accept this community's religious faith precisely
as relevant to the pursuit of new truth. The perception of
relevancy must, moreover, be clear and strong; students

must necessarily take a further step, *freely and generously* to accept the responsibilities which all perceived truth necessarily imposes—particularly the religious-faith insights of the Catholic academic community. The religious development program on the Catholic campus must teach students that "truth involves its own obedience," as do justice, love, and freedom; that the sincere search for new truth requires a personal and corporate living of truth already known. It is obvious enough that student religious development, so conceived, cannot be the sole responsibility of campus chaplains, committees, or scattered dedicated clerics and laymen. The religious development program must be an outgrowth of the Catholic university's academic nature and mission.

In any discussion of religious development programs for Catholic university campuses, therefore, the basic consideration must be the spirit and character of the Catholic university itself. Is the university seeking to "function as a true university"? Does it have an awareness of and project an excitement about the importance of applying faith-insights to the quest for new truth in the context of the larger academe? Is it attempting to exemplify in its own corporate life the qualities of lay spirituality which it attempts to communicate to students? These are not isolated questions. The Catholic university which is applying its faith-insights to the search for new truth, which clearly perceives both its dependence upon and its mission within the larger academe, must almost necessarily adopt a spirit and character which will communicate to students the qualities which are essential to lay spirituality. It is, therefore, the total spirit and character of the Catholic university, particularly as the Catholic university perceives itself in relation to academe, that is of first importance to the religious development programs of Catholic universities.

D. AN EXCITING PLACE, AND DANGEROUS

Michael P. Walsh, S.J., has been quoted earlier as saying that the Catholic university must become "the place
where the Church does its thinking." Although neither the
Second Vatican Council nor any pope has ever explicitly
declared that the Church will in the future do its thinking
on Catholic university campuses, the ideals for the development of Catholic laymen expressed by Pope John and the
Council presuppose circumstances which can only be found
on Catholic campuses. The Council says, for instance, that
the people of God as a whole, "from the bishops down to
the last member of the laity," clings "to the faith once de-
livered to the saints, penetrates it more deeply by accurate
insights, and applies it more thoroughly to life." [8] To provide the conditions in which the most educated segment of
God's people will penetrate the faith by more accurate
insights and search for its more thorough application to
life is the precise mission of the Catholic university. If
these functions of the people of God represent in any way
the Church doing her thinking, then the Church will indeed
do much of her thinking on Catholic campuses in the years
ahead.

The Council anticipates no challenge to the teaching
authority of the Holy Father or of the bishops teaching in
communion with the Roman Pontiff when the people of
God seek to penetrate the faith more deeply or to apply it
more thoroughly to life. Quite the contrary: the Council
calls for a "living exchange" of the whole Church with
diverse cultures of people.

To promote such an exchange, the Church requires special

[8] *Documents, Vatican II,* "Dogmatic Constitution on the Church"
§ 12 (pp. 29-30).

help, particularly in our day, when things are changing very rapidly and the ways of thinking are exceedingly various. She must rely on those who live in the world, are versed in different institutions and specialties, and grasp their innermost significance in the eyes of both believers and unbelievers.[9]

The Council obviously has in mind an exchange where truth will be passed up as well as down, an exchange which can best be accomplished by educated men on Catholic campuses.

Although the Council fathers may never have adverted to the fact, it is inevitable that the Catholic university play a more than instrumental role in this "living exchange" by which "revealed truth [will be] more deeply penetrated, better understood and set forth to advantage." [10] Christians are exhorted by the Council to join "with the rest of men in the search for truth, and for the genuine solution to the numerous problems that arise in the life of individuals and from social relationships." [11] Must not this exchange take place paradigmatically on Catholic campuses?

There is something quite exciting about all of this. If Catholic campuses truly become through this living exchange "the place where the Church meets the world and the world meets the Church," Catholic campuses will not be just interesting and exciting places but quite important ideological forums.[12]

[9] *Ibid.*, "Pastoral Constitution on the Church in the Modern World" § 44 (p. 246).

[10] *Ibid.*

[11] *Ibid.*, § 16 (p. 214).

[12] It is difficult to comprehend all that this development will mean to Catholic higher education in the years ahead. One is startled upon examining the extremes of the change. Just a century ago small Catholic colleges prized their remote locations where students could be carefully isolated from ideas which were alien and at times hostile to Catholic teaching. Now Catholic campuses are to serve as the forum where the insights of religious faith are

"A good university," it is sometimes said, "is a dangerous place." How dangerous will it be for students to witness
and participate in the dialogue and argument which will
take place at Catholic universities if Catholic campuses
become ideological forums where the Church honestly ex-
changes insights with the secular world and the world with
the Church? Will not exposure to the *living* expression of
ideas which cannot be fully reconciled with long-cherished
and even sacred religious and societal values be a danger
to students? *Living* expression is essential to a full and true
exchange. The danger factor must honestly be weighed.

The danger of living in the midst of such a controversial
atmosphere could be considerable to students who have an
immature, simplistic concept of their Catholic faith. Students who have not learned to critically examine their own
religious convictions in the light of the equally sincere convictions of other men would very likely be harmed. There
will be, therefore, a type of academic religious maturity
and competence required of students on Catholic campuses
in the future such as was not required in the past. It must
be the function of broadened and intensified religious development programs on Catholic campuses to develop this
religious maturity and competence. Unless this is achieved,

---

critically applied to all secular knowledge and ideas, and where
secular knowledge and ideas are to be critically applied to the
faith's most sacred doctrines and insights.

The change is, as a matter of fact, already occurring and is
already far advanced on some campuses. Catholic university libraries no longer lock off books expressing ideas contrary to Catholic
faith and morals. Speakers coming to Catholic campuses are no
longer carefully selected for their orthodoxy. Moreover, all of this
is occurring with an ecumenical spirit of friendly exchange and
academic perceptiveness. On Catholic campuses the Church is
already saying, "Here are our insights; what are yours? Here is
what we have to offer you; what do you have to offer us?" The
living exchange is already taking place.

Catholic campuses of the future could be very dangerous places for Catholic students.

Before discussing the elements of student religious maturity and competence, some perspective might be given to the problem of danger by regarding it from a different aspect. Given the signs of the times, particularly as they pertain to students on Catholic university campuses, what dangers will result if students perceive efforts to *shelter* and *protect* them from ideas which, in the judgment of administrators and faculty, are considered alien and hostile to the Catholic faith? What dangers will result if Catholic students are not allowed to participate *now* in the living exchange which they consider essential to the university's functioning as a true university? How dangerous will it be if students are *not* allowed and encouraged to form their own critical judgments with respect to matters which they perceive as vital to themselves and to their own future society? What dangers are involved in *not* allowing students on Catholic campuses to hear the *living* expression of ideas which elsewhere in academe are taken seriously by competent scholars?

In other words, just how safe will the religious faith of students be on "safe" Catholic campuses in the years ahead? There is serious reason to believe that the protected campus will constitute a far greater danger to the religious faith of students than a campus which provides exposure to an honest, forthright confrontation with all ideas current in the larger academe. Catholic students have a legitimate desire to be "where the action is," not just because the action is interesting and exciting but because the action provided by a living exchange of important ideas is essential to academic development. The safety factor in future Catholic education, therefore, cannot be provided by restricting the living exchange on Catholic campuses to selected, relatively safe ideas, but must be achieved by providing students with an academically mature religious competence to participate in the discussion of *all* ideas that are current in academe. Campus religious development programs can remove the danger from future Catholic university education only by providing students with a competence to apply critically and academically the faith-insights of the Catholic university community to the intellectual action of the day.

E. ACADEMIC RELIGIOUS COMPETENCE

What qualities are essential to students who seek to become active members in a Catholic academic community which is functioning not only as a true university but as a forum for a living exchange of ideas and insights between the Church and secular society? An exhaustive listing of such qualities is impossible. Some, however, are obvious enough. In the consideration of the qualities which will be suggested, it is interesting to note that in almost every case they are essentially qualities which students can develop only by becoming active members in a Catholic university community. It is almost inconceivable that they should be acquired in any other manner. Once again, therefore, let it be said that the religious development program on a Catholic university campus is a total university responsibility which has as its goal the incorporation of students into an academic community which is alive and vibrant with religious faith.

The basic quality required for academic religious competence pertains to the attitude which the academic community must have toward religious faith. It is not enough that students attending a Catholic university possess religious faith. Unless they perceive their faith as a means for seeking new truth their faith is of little consequence in the university community. In other words, in the academic community faith must be perceived not as a goal to be attained but as a means for seeking new truth. Religious faith may, and should, be deepened as a result of the university experience and new faith-insights should be achieved; but this deepened faith and these new faith-insights are important to the academic community primarily because they provide additional means for seeking further truth and still deeper faith-insights. Paradoxically, truth itself, however attained, is important in the academic community primarily because it serves as a means to search for further truth. That students have this academic attitude toward religious faith is a basic quality of religious academic competence in the university community.

This first quality, it might be observed, sharply distinguishes the Catholic university from the secularist-humanist academic community which today is so frequently characterized by agnosticism and skepticism. In the current secular-humanist view the final academic goal can only be "subjective truth" or perennially reversible convictions. This cannot be the final goal in the Catholic academic community's search for truth. First, the Catholic academic community respects the possibility of man's attaining truths which are objective and irreversible. Second, as a result of faith-insights the Catholic university community acknowledges certain truths, e.g., the Triune God and Jesus Christ as God-man, which are beyond human comprehension. Catholic scholars must certainly seek a deeper and more penetrating understanding of truths respected in the Catholic tradition as already known, but again, academically only as a means to achieving further truth.

Because the Catholic scholar seeks ultimately for truths which are objective and irreversible and regards personal understanding only as a means toward achieving this goal, he must perceive the spiritual dimensions of his dependence on the academic community in his search for new truth. The most profound faith-insights are a community achievement. It is the religious insights of the Catholic university community which are of greatest importance to academe. It is not enough, therefore, to say that the Catholic university corporately represents a long-respected tradition in academe and that it corporately seeks to deepen its own understanding of that tradition. Theoretically at least, this could be accomplished by a group of competent secular scholars on a public campus. The Catholic university seeks to be something more. It perceives religious faith as a living community experience where the intersubjectivity of believers, producing a deep mutual respect and understanding, develops a further, living, continuing faith interaction.[13] In the Catholic university community the personal faith of each individual interacts with the faith of others. As a result of this interaction, individual faith is reinforced and deepened while community faith unfolds in a living, ever-deepening tradition.[14] It is this living, interacting faith tradition which produces its own faith-insights. These are

[13] "The importance of faith's intersubjective character can hardly be over-emphasized. Christian belief is not a subject-object relation, but a subject-subject relation: the 'I-thou' of accepted or rejected brother love. Theological personalists wrongly speak of two inter-subjectivities, a horizontal one between men and a vertical one between man and God. This false division fails to take into account two insights. First, the inter-subjectivity between men is itself open toward God; brother love is the context of salvific love. Second, the specifically Christian subject of the man-God relationship is not man as an individual but man in his oneness with all men. What is most personal in man occurs in brotherly love" (Metz, Johannes B., "Unbelief and Believers," *Theology Digest*, Autumn, 1967).

[14] "It is first of all through the Christian family that Christianity appears as a tradition and not simply as a personal choice" (Jean Daniélou, S.J., "What Good Is Institutional Christianity?" *The Critic*, June-July, 1967). In the Catholic academic community Christianity is more important *"as a tradition"* than "simply as a personal choice."

the insights which are applied by the Catholic academic community to the search for new truth in academe.[15]

Because the tradition of faith as expressed by the Catholic *community* is so important, there is a special academically appropriate humility required of students at a Catholic university. Hopefully, students in the future will be primarily motivated to attend Catholic universities because they feel they can best achieve an understanding of life's meaning in the context of the living faith tradition which exists only on Catholic campuses. In order to be incorporated into this living tradition students must be open to accepting it as their own—*freely*. The community has a responsibility to require of students everything that is essential to their achieving this incorporation.[16] The student, for his part, must accept these requirements with an appropriate academic humility. Questioning, challenging and probing even the tradition itself is not in the least inappropriate to student humility. Quite the contrary: such actions are necessary preliminaries to an informed, free acceptance of the tradition. The academic dimension of humility requires only an openness to the religious tradition of the

[15] The importance of the liturgy in giving (literally) life to the community expression of this tradition cannot be overemphasized. Liturgical renewal on the university campus must seek a more explicit expression of the academic aspects of the religious tradition which the Catholic university brings to academe.

[16] The frequently heard student argument that "nothing of educational or academic value can come from what is compulsory" is rejected as pedagogically unsound. The academic competence in philosophy and theology required for mature university dialogue cannot be presumed of young students newly arrived on the Catholic university campus. The Catholic university has a responsibility to require whatever is essential to students' moving toward a mature competence in philosophy and theology. If nothing of educational advantage or academic value results from such requirements, the fault lies elsewhere, not in the fact of their being required.

community as it manifests its academic relevance. With
respect to religious requirements, therefore, the university
community is well warned to regard students "not as bottles
to be filled but as lamps to be lit." The lamp is easily ex-
tinguished by religious requirements which appear to students as unimportant for and irrelevant to the academic
mission of the university.

The human spirit must be cultivated in such a way that there
results a growth in its ability to wonder, to understand, to
contemplate, to make personal judgments, and to develop a
religious, moral and social sense.[17]

As the truth is discovered it is by a personal assent that men
are to adhere to it.[18]

It is almost superfluous to add that mutual respect is an
essential quality for academic development. It is mentioned
here only because an especially high degree of mutual respect should characterize a Christian academic community.

Respect and love ought to be extended to those who think or
act differently than we do in social, political, and religious
matters, too. In fact, the more deeply we come to understand

A more difficult problem arises with respect to religious exercises
which the Catholic university might require, e.g., retreats. The
university might wisely determine that certain religious exercises,
such as retreats, are essential to students' being effectively incorporated into the religious spirit and character of the Catholic
academic community. Again, the problem concerns not the fact
that the religious exercises are required but rather their manifest
relevance to the academic purpose and mission of the Catholic
university community. If this relevance is not apparent—or worse,
if the community does not project to students an academic purpose and mission which presumes important religious aspects—
the required religious exercises will most likely arouse a justified
student resentment.

[17] *Documents, Vatican II*, "Pastoral Constitution on the Church
in the Modern World" § 59 (p. 265).

[18] *Ibid.*, "Declaration on Religious Freedom" § 3 (p. 681).

their ways of thinking through such courtesy and love, the more easily will we be able to enter into dialogue with them.[19]

Mutual respect by no means precludes disagreement. It is not only normal but healthy that there be disagreement in the academic community, even when at times this results in serious tensions. Dialogue and argument are essential means for achieving truth in academe. "From the conflict of minds trying to be friendly comes truth." It is not just from the conflict, however, but equally from the friendliness that truth results. Friendliness in the academic community projects a "trying to understand." It is saying: "Even though we strongly disagree, there are certainly elements of truth in what each of us is saying. What is your background, your approach to this problem, the reasons behind what you are saying? You see this thing so differently than I. Help me to understand your view."

Truth is to be sought after in a manner proper to the dignity of the human person and his social nature. The inquiry is to be free, carried on with the aid of teaching or instruction, communication, and dialogue. In the course of these, men explain to one another the truth they have discovered, or think they have discovered, in order thus to assist one another in the quest for truth.[20]

Perhaps the quality of religious academic competence most difficult for Catholic students to understand as they are incorporated into the Catholic university community is that of the human person and his social nature. The inquiry is to faith that the Church must *teach* in order to guide and unify the people of God. It is equally basic that this teaching function is exercised by the Holy Father, as Vicar of Christ, and by the bishops when they speak in unison with

[19] *Ibid.*, "Pastoral Constitution on the Church in the Modern World" § 28 (p. 227).
[20] *Ibid.*, "Declaration on Religious Freedom" § 3 (pp. 680-681).

the Roman Pontiff. There are many areas of Christian life in which tensions will always exist. It is normal enough, moreover, that from time to time tensions will arise between the magisterium of the Church and the Catholic university. These latter tensions will be lessened, however, as in the years ahead the magisterium and the Catholic university, seeking to function as a true university, come to a deeper understanding and appreciation of the interdependence of their respective roles within the Church. The following understandings are particularly important:

First, in every society there is an *appropriate* freedom. Freedom is never absolute but is always limited by the responsibilities which each society embraces as it perceives the demands of truth. Within the Church, therefore, the magisterium *per se* imposes no limits on the Catholic university in its search for truth. Limitations on the Catholic university's search for truth can only be imposed by the responsibilities which truth requires as perceived in the Catholic society—i.e., as taught by the magisterium. This limitation of freedom by truth as perceived in the Catholic society is appropriate to any university which considers itself Catholic.

It is important to note that limitations determined by the responsibilities which truth imposes cannot frustrate a university's functioning as a true university. Quite the contrary: such limitations provide for a more effective community freedom by opening up possibilities of an academic creative interdependence in the community's search for new truth.

Second, truth itself, by whomever it is taught, imposes no restrictions on the means for achieving further truths which are proper to academe. Just as dialogue and argument are proper to the academic society, so is the questioning and probing of truth already known. In its questioning

and probing function the Catholic university must allow
the expression of all ideas that are taken seriously in the
larger academic society even though some of these ideas
may be contrary to "the teaching of the Church." To allow
such expression is not a disloyalty in the academic context
but a means which is absolutely essential to studying the
Church's teaching in full critical context and to penetrating
its deeper meanings. The magisterium must respect, therefore, not just the ideal of the true university to pursue new
truth, but must honor as well the means which are appropriate to the academic society.

Third, the magisterium must respect the function of the
university as critic of all the societies which it seeks to
serve. Serving as social critic is a long-respected function
of the academic community. In performing this function
within the Church the Catholic university serves the Church
by assisting her to perceive truth about herself. In the case
of the Catholic university this responsibility to serve as
critic would apply to the magisterium itself even in the
exercise of its teaching function.[21]

For the Christian University's perennial task has been to insure
the awareness, the talent, and the instruments whereby the
body corporate of Christianity must do its thinking, bring its
faith to self-reflective understanding, and devise appropriate
lines of action in and upon both Church and world. The
Catholic University represents, accordingly, a most appropriate
organ for the Church's perennial function of self-study and
reflection. The University must be free to analyze, therefore,
and analyze not only false and ungrounded attacks upon the

---

[21] An instance of the Catholic university's exercising this function
of critic to the magisterium in its teaching role would be John
Courtney Murray's suggestion with respect to the birth-control
issue, that "the Church reached for too much certainty too soon,
and went too far" (McCloskey, Paul W., "The CAIP, What Is
Its Future?" *Commonweal,* November 17, 1967, p. 195).

faith, but formulations, defenses and practical orientations which in a phrase St. Thomas used centuries ago, only bring the faith into derision. This critical function she [the Catholic university] must exercise competently, responsibly—but frankly and honestly as well.[22]

Fourth, truth as perceived in the Church imposes a special humility which is appropriate to the Catholic university. While great freedom of expression must be allowed on Catholic campuses, and while the university's function as critic must be acknowledged, it would be quite inappropriate that the personal convictions of an individual or of a group be advanced as though they were on a par with the clear teaching of the magisterium. Moreover, it is an expression of the humility appropriate to the Catholic university that Catholic scholars deeply understand their indebtedness to the teaching Church for the unique faith-insights they bring to academe.[23]

Fifth, all Catholics must understand more perceptively the role of the Church in the modern world as "servant," particularly as this applies to the Catholic university and

---

[22] Arrupe, *op. cit.,* p. 26.
[23] The indebtedness of the Catholic scholar (and of the Catholic university) to the Church precisely as *teacher* is more far-reaching than the student is likely readily to realize. The *academic* implications of St. Paul's observation of man's moral ambivalence is not easily dismissed: "I cannot understand my own behavior. I fail to carry out things I want to do, and I find myself doing the things I hate" (Romans, 7:25, *The Jerusalem Bible* translation). Given man's propensity to rationalize his behavior, how important is the teaching Church to the Catholic scholar in his pursuit of truth which is objective and irreversible? How important would Christian revelation be to the scholar if it did no more than caution him with respect to his personal convictions, however sincerely held? Humility is an essential quality of all scholars. Humility manifested as loyalty to, and a deep respect for, the teaching Church is not only appropriate to the Catholic scholar but essential to his academic religious competence in the Catholic university community.

its mission within academe. Neither the Church nor the Catholic university itself has in the past thought of the Catholic academic community as serving academe. Until very recent times small Catholic colleges not only sought ideological isolation but deliberately ignored the larger academic society. Now the Catholic university, while embracing academe as an ally in the quest for new truth, must fulfill a "servant" role within academe. All Catholics must understand that if the Catholic university is to fulfill this new mission it must enjoy the freedoms which are appropriate to a true university. The quality of loyalty to the Church will be achieved by the Catholic university in proportion to its being allowed to serve the Church as a competent and respected member of academe.

CONCLUSION

The argument has been long. The conclusion will be brief. So much has been said about the Catholic university, as a respected corporate member of academe, applying community faith-insights to the problems that face mankind. The emphasis has been on faith. Respect and love have been mentioned as qualities necessary to a "friendly" exchange of ideas. What of the third great Christian virtue, that of hope?

When all is said and done, perhaps the greatest service the Catholic university can provide academe is to communicate to the larger academic society its spirit of hope, its spirit of realistic optimism that is so important to Catholic spirituality. The larger academic society sorely needs today a spirit of hope and vision. Viktor Frankl writes of the failure of modern man to perceive a purpose and meaning in life. If the Catholic university communicates only its vision and spirit of hope to the many, so very many, men of good will in academe, her mission will in large part be fulfilled:

. . . the future of humanity lies in the hands of those who are strong enough to provide coming generations with reasons for living and hoping.[24]

[24] *Documents, Vatican II*, "Pastoral Constitution on the Church in the Modern World" § 31 (p. 230).

PART TWO
RIGHTS AND FREEDOMS OF STUDENTS

I

A Report and Commentary on

the "Joint Statement on the Rights

and Freedoms of Students" *

A. BRIEF HISTORICAL PERSPECTIVE

IN OCTOBER, 1960, the Council of the American Association of University Professors (AAUP) authorized the formation of a standing Committee S, to be entitled, Committee on Faculty Responsibility for the Academic Freedom of Students. Committee S was commissioned to develop

* June, 1968; revised.

"positions and policies" with respect to student rights and freedoms which would be appropriate to college and university communities in our American society. It is important to note that Committee S was an offshoot of AAUP's Committee A on Academic Freedom and Tenure for faculty. Hopefully, Committee S would develop a document with respect to student academic freedom which would complement AAUP's 1940 "Statement of Principles of Academic Freedom and Tenure." The wonder is that the task of formulating principles and policies with respect to student academic rights and freedoms on college and university campuses in the United States was so long delayed.

Throughout the nineteenth century the two complementary aspects of academic freedom, *Lehrfreiheit* pertaining to faculty and *Lernfreiheit* pertaining to students, underwent a parallel development in German universities. Many of the American scholars who studied in German universities during this period returned to the United States strong supporters of *Lehrfreiheit* which provided teachers in German universities the freedom openly to teach and publish the results of their scholarly research in the fields of their particular competence without fear of government reprisals. As a result of the German university influence on American academe, the concept of academic freedom for faculty gradually began to gain acceptance in the United States in the years following the Civil War. American academicians found strong support for the innovation in the writings of Thomas Jefferson.

For a number of reasons the German concept of *Lernfreiheit*, guaranteeing to students analogous freedoms of inquiry and expression, was not introduced into American colleges and universities at this same period. Williamson treats this anomaly quite extensively, concluding that

the relative immaturity in age and behavior of American students, faculty preoccupation with problems of disruptive and

riotous student behavior and discipline, traditional denomina-
tional fervor and piety, crushing financial poverty—these and
other conditions in the American college during the late
eighteenth and early nineteenth centuries in a real sense pre-
cluded the granting to our students of the much-vaunted academic freedom so firmly established in Germanic culture and
tradition.[1]

Another reason why *Lernfreiheit* was not transferred with
Lehrfreiheit from the German to the American educational
tradition at this early period was the need of American
society for a stable form of education which strongly
reinforced the stern virtues of early American economic,
political, social, and religious life. American adult society
from the colonial period to well into the twentieth century
simply would not tolerate or support an educational system
which did not sustain every aspect of the prevailing American way of life. The nation was too youthful and enthu-
siastic to question its own values.

One of the first acts of the newly established United
States National Student Association (USNSA) in 1948 was
to issue a Basic Policy Declaration with respect to the
implications of academic freedom for students on American
campuses. The Declaration spoke of

the right and responsibility of the student to participate fully
in independent inquiry and criticism. It is his right to question, criticize, and dissent from ideas with which he comes
in contact, and to hold and advocate his personal beliefs free
from all pressures which tend to restrict the student in his
pursuit of knowledge.[2]

Although perhaps not intentionally, the USNSA Declaration on Academic Freedom in 1948 enunciated the same

[1] Williamson, E. G., *Student Personnel Services in Colleges and
Universities,* New York: McGraw-Hill, 1961, p. 291.
[2] United States National Student Association, *Codification of
Policy,* 1967-8, p. 39.

basic principles for student academic freedom as those already accepted in German universities for well over a century.

It is generally felt that the U.S. Senate investigations of Senator Joseph McCarthy during the nineteen fifties retarded the cause of student (and faculty) academic freedom in the United States for a decade. Even during this period, however, events were taking place which set the stage for a more thorough consideration of student rights and freedoms once McCarthy's influence was terminated. Following the Second World War higher education became a possibility for ever-increasing numbers of young Americans. College education was no longer considered a privilege in American society. It became a necessity to economic and social advancement. As a result the arbitrary dismissal of students from colleges and universities became an acute issue. In 1957 Seavey wrote his now-famous article in the *Harvard Law Review* in which he complained:

It is shocking that officials of a state educational institution, which can function properly only if our freedoms are preserved, should not understand the elementary principles of fair play. It is equally shocking to find that a court supports them in denying to a student the protection given to a pickpocket.[3]

The stage was set for a full consideration of student rights and freedoms as they should be honored on American college and university campuses.

In 1961 the American Civil Liberties Union (ACLU) published its first full statement on "Academic Freedom and Civil Liberties of Students in Colleges and Universities." The original ACLU statement was revised in 1963. During the same period state and federal courts began to take a stronger position with respect to the right of students not to have their college education terminated by

[3] Seavey, *op. cit.*, p. 1407.

the arbitrary acts of university officers. During the early 'sixties a number of cases involving the arbitrary dismissal of students because of their off-campus participation in the civil rights movement were decided by the courts in favor of the students. By the time AAUP's Committee S began its considerations of student academic freedom, therefore, a considerable body of literature, statements and legislation had already accumulated. It was the hope of Committee S to bring this material to a cohesive unity.

B. FROM COMMITTEE S TO A "JOINT STATEMENT"

During the period 1961–1963, AAUP's Committee S worked out its initial statement on student academic freedoms. The Autumn, 1964, issue of the AAUP *Bulletin* carried the first published draft with the following careful qualification:

The statement which follows has been prepared by the Association's Committee on Faculty Responsibility for the Academic Freedom of Students. Since it has not yet been formally approved by the Association's Council, the statement is to be looked upon as tentative—an expression of the Committee's views rather than of Association policy.[4]

Comment was requested to assist in further revision. In October, 1965, the Chairman of Committee S, Dr. Phillip Monypenny, reported to the AAUP Council that he had received many comments from administrative officers, faculty members, and students with respect to the first published draft of the statement. He presented a revised draft which the Council accepted "in principle" and approved for publication in the Winter, 1965, issue of the *Bulletin*. This second published draft was introduced by the following comment:

[4]AAUP *Bulletin*, "Statement on Faculty Responsibility for the Academic Freedom of Students," Autumn, 1964, p. 254.

The statement which follows has been approved by the Council in principle but remains a tentative, rather than a fixed, statement of Association policy. The Council has also authorized Committee S to initiate discussions with representatives of other interested national organizations in the hope that these efforts might result in the formulation of a joint statement on student rights and responsibilities. These discussions will commence this winter.[5]

Informal meetings were held with representatives of other interested organizations during the spring of 1966. As these meetings progressed the wide disparity of views with respect to student rights and freedoms became ever more apparent. In November, 1966, Committee S sponsored a special meeting in Washington to determine whether or not enough consensus existed to make it feasible to consider further the possibility of developing a *joint* statement. Four other national organizations, representing the conspectus of American academe, were each invited to send five delegates to the meeting: the Association of American Colleges (AAC) representing college and university presidents; the National Association of Student Personnel Administrators (NASPA) and the National Association of Women Deans and Counselors (NAWDC) representing student personnel; the USNSA representing students. Five other national educational associations sent observers to the meeting.[6]

The views expressed by the respective delegations at this November meeting indeed demonstrated the wide disparity of opinions that existed in the academic society with respect to student rights and freedoms. USNSA representatives advocated a complete student autonomy within the

[5] AAUP *Bulletin,* "Statement on the Academic Freedom of Students," Winter, 1965, p. 447.

[6] American Council on Education, Association of American Universities, Association of Higher Education, Association of State Colleges and Universities, and the American College Association.

university community with student voice in all other university business which in any way touched upon student
curricular or co-curricular interests. At the opposite pole
the AAC delegates insisted that the wide diversity of educational goals in American higher education, however these
goals affected student life, should be protected and encouraged. NAWDC severely criticized the AAUP document
both for its excessive legalism and for failing to define the
relationship of students to the university upon which its
approach to student rights and freedoms was based.
NASPA delegates felt that the student representatives were
demanding freedom without accountability. From all
quarters the AAUP proposal was questioned for the inade-
quacy of its treatment of student rights and freedoms in
the section where faculty should be most concerned—"in
the classroom."

While the November, 1966, meeting proved for some a
source of great discouragement, the outspoken character
of the sessions probably proved the salvation of the project.
The polarity of views was clearly exposed. It was apparent
that if a joint statement was to be produced in the foreseeable future it would have to be based, where possible, on
present compromise and allow for future development
through evolving understandings. Almost immediately after
the meeting each of the sponsoring organizations appointed
a single member to a smaller committee which was charged
with drafting a statement that would be mutually acceptable.[7] During the spring of 1967 members of the drafting
committee corresponded and met informally. In June,
1967, this smaller group agreed to a final draft of a "Joint

[7] Members of the Joint Drafting Committee: Dr. Phillip Mony-
penny (AAUP), Dr. Harry D. Gideonse (AAC), Mr. Earle Clifford
(NASPA), Dr. Ann Bromley (NAWDC); Mr. Edward Schwartz
(USNSA). Mr. Robert Van Waes (AAUP) and Dr. Peter H.
Armacost (AAC) served as consultants to the Committee.

Statement on the Rights and Freedoms of Students." Each of the five delegates was then asked to propose the Joint Statement to his respective organization at their annual national conference for final endorsement.

A separate resolution, proposed by AAC and accepted by the final drafting committee, was a source of some confusion during the endorsement period. The resolution reads as follows:

It was agreed that, before becoming party to any joint statement on student rights and responsibilities, the Association should insist that all the parties to such an agreement should undertake:

1. To set up machinery for continuing joint interpretation of the policies and procedures recommended in the agreement;
2. To consult with each other before setting up any machinery for investigating complaints of alleged violation of the agreement;
3. To request the regional accrediting associations to embody the principles of the agreement in their standards for accreditation.

This resolution, labeled "Enforcement," was incorporated into the document as proposed to the USNSA Student Congress. It does not appear, however, in the official USNSA *1967–8 Codification of Policy* where the Joint Statement is given in full. The AAUP *Bulletin,* Winter, 1967, does not carry the text of the resolution but obviously refers to it in its introduction to a printing of the final draft of the Statement.

The multilateral approach which produced the Joint Statement was also projected, on a tentative basis, to the complicated matter of implementation and enforcement, with the drafting committee recommending (*a*) joint efforts to promote acceptance of the new standards on the institutional level, (*b*) the establishment of machinery to facilitate continuing joint interpretation, (c) joint consultation before setting up any machinery for mediating disputes or investigating complaints, and (d) joint approaches to regional accrediting agencies to seek embodiment of the new principles in standards of accreditation.[8]

Although AAC, NASPA and NAWDC did not include the resolution in copies of the document circulated to their memberships, all three explicitly refer to the first two provisions of the resolution in their respective endorsements. While the resolution, therefore, cannot be considered a part of the Joint Statement itself, its first two provisions must be considered an essential condition of its future interpretation and implementation.

The endorsements of the Joint Statement by the five sponsoring organizations provide not only interesting commentary on the compromise nature of the document but also material which is essential to its understanding and implementation on various campuses. USNSA was the first of the five organizations to hold a national meeting. In late August, Edward Schwartz, President of USNSA, proposed adoption at the National Student Congress. In his printed presentation Schwartz emphasized that the Joint Statement represented a "minimal document." "Institutional diversity," he stated, "is no justification for provisions affecting free inquiry and free expression." [9] The tenor of the USNSA endorsement is clear. Its approach to future clarifications, implementations, and enforcements is indicated.

In late October, 1967, the AAUP Council endorsed the Joint Statement "unanimously and enthusiastically." In an accompanying resolution the AAUP Council expressed its views with respect to the non-academic character of the

[8] AAUP *Bulletin*, "Joint Statement on Rights and Freedoms of Students," Winter, 1967, p. 365.
[9] Schwartz, Edward, *Joint Statement on the Academic Freedoms of Students, A Summary and An Analysis*, USNSA, July, 1967, p. 6.

disruptive tactics currently all too familiar on American campuses.

In view of some recent events, the Council deems it important to state its conviction that action by individuals or groups to prevent speakers invited to the campus from speaking, to disrupt the operations of the institutions in the course of demonstrations, or to obstruct and restrain other members of the academic community and campus visitors by physical force is destructive of the pursuit of learning in a free society. All components of the academic community are under a strong obligation to protect its processes from these tactics.[10]

The most interesting and perhaps the most crucial of the endorsements was that passed by AAC in their January, 1968, national meeting. In November, 1967, AAC President, Dr. Richard E. Sullivan, circulated to the entire membership a resolution approved by the Executive Committee which provided for immediate endorsement of the Joint Statement at the January meeting with nine "explicit understandings for clarification." Reactions to the resolution were immediate and strong. Objections were raised that endorsement of the Joint Statement "would foster a sense of irresponsibility" since the Statement showed "little or no concern for administrative freedom and ultimate responsibility" and so "would reverse this long-established method of administering institutional affairs." In December the AAC Resolutions Committee agreed to a substitute resolution with an alternative. The substitute resolution would have provided for official AAC endorsement after a year of observation. The alternate resolution made no provision for ultimate endorsement. At the AAC meeting in January considerable support for the original November resolution developed when the twenty-eight presidents of the Jesuit colleges and universities unanimously endorsed the Joint

[10] The AAUP Council resolution, passed at the October meeting, 1967, is not carried in the AAUP *Bulletin*.

Statement with two clarifications in an independent action just previous to the AAC general meeting. The Jesuit endorsement was followed by that of the College and University Executive Committee of the National Catholic Education Association. An amended form of the November resolution, providing for immediate endorsement with ten clarifications, was ultimately passed by an overwhelming majority at the final AAC business session on January 17.

It is important to comment on the nature of the ten "explicit understandings for clarification" which were incorporated into the AAC endorsement. By no means can these understandings be construed as amendments to the Joint Statement either weakening or providing essential changes in the document itself.[11] Three members of the final drafting committee for the Joint Statement and one of its consultants were in attendance at the AAC meeting and were actively working for its adoption *with the clarifications,* each attesting that the clarifications expressed the mind of the final drafting committee.[12] The AAC clarifications can be said, therefore, to constitute valid understandings of the Joint Statement for interpretation and implementation on various campuses.

In early April, 1968, both NASPA and NAWDC endorsed the Joint Statement at their annual national conferences. Both endorsements repeat many of the clarifications of the AAC endorsement. One special point in the NASPA endorsement provides an insight for understanding and interpreting the document. The Joint Statement is

[11] The "explicit understandings for clarification" of the AAC endorsement in no way alter the principles proposed in the Joint Statement. For the most part they concern details of implementation.

[12] Present at the AAC meeting: Dr. Harry D. Gideonse (AAC), Mr. Earle Clifford (NASPA), Dr. Peter H. Armacost (AAC), and Mr. Edward Schwartz (USNSA). All agreed that the AAC "understandings for clarification" in no way violate the intentions of the final drafting committee.

said *to define important principles* and *to describe possible practices*. The principles embodied in the document, the NASPA endorsement asserts, should be implemented on all campuses. The particular means of implementing these principles, the practices mentioned in the Joint Statement, need not be followed precisely as described in the document, but may vary from campus to campus. The distinction between principles, which are defined, and practices, which are described, is extremely important to understanding and implementing the Joint Statement.

C. BASIC PRINCIPLES OF THE JOINT STATEMENT

The dichotomy between early American education and the type of education which is currently evolving on our American college and university campuses cannot be overestimated. Basically the difference lies in the role which the student is expected to play in his own education. In early American education the student was expected to play an almost passive role in the educational process. The student was taught. His character was formed. He was expected uncritically to absorb the knowledge, wisdom, and values of the society in which he lived and, after graduation, to identify with its accepted goals. For a variety of reasons students today will no longer accept this passive role. They insist on playing a more self-determining role in their own education. Moreover, they insist on the right to criticize openly both the content of their education and the values of the society that this education reinforces. The Joint Statement reflects this change. It reacts strongly against the mode of earlier American education, endorsing the present trend which would provide students with a maximum opportunity to assume an increased personal responsibility for their own self-development.

In promoting an increased student responsibility for self-development the Joint Statement enunciates the student right to learn with its complementary freedoms of inquiry and expression. A further factor is involved. If students are to assume a realistic responsibility for their personal self-development they must be allowed, far more than in the past, to play an influential role in determining the circumstances in which they are to pursue their educational self-development. The Joint Statement, therefore, provides that students play a more active part in the formulation of institutional policies which directly affect student development.

Such principles undoubtedly seem not only revolutionary but irresponsible to educators who are oriented to the methods of early American education. And, indeed, if the pendulum is allowed to swing to the opposite extreme such forebodings are not improper. Williamson comments on the dangers of such an over-reaction.

Sometimes discussion of academic freedom for students leads to advocacy of oversimplified and absolutistic solutions. Until some judicious practices were introduced on campuses, absolutistic repression of student behavior and student liberties were given thorough trial. Its gradual, but too-long-delayed, abandonment was followed by a reactive attempt to define the administration out of the sphere of responsibility for student behavior and affairs. This was the age in which students, with some administrative and faculty support, sought for an area of complete independence and autonomy. It was advocated by some that the institution turn over to the students the management of their own affairs and leave them to their own devices, assuming no responsibility for what they did outside of the classroom. In support of such independence of action, some advocates referred to academic freedom in European universities, especially in German universities. . . . And, in further support of autonomy, an analogy was frequently drawn between the free enterprise in ideas on a campus and the free discussion of Hyde Park or Pershing Square.[13]

It is ironical that Williamson discusses these ideas as though they were of a former "age." They constitute the basic issues of student power at the present time.

The Joint Statement does not advocate turning over our American campuses to students. However, it does endorse a concept of community responsibility in which students, along with administration and faculty, are encouraged to play a more determining role in the formulation of institutional policy. The Joint Statement does not advocate an autonomy for the student sector of the university community. However, it does endorse the principle that a college or university community allow students whatever freedoms of inquiry and expression are necessary for students to develop an independent capacity to search for truth. The Joint Statement does not advocate an absolute freedom for students. However, it does hold that whatever restrictions an academic community places on students must be reasonable in terms of educational goals. The Joint Statement does not advocate that universities abdicate all responsibility for student development outside the classroom. However, it does maintain that the development of students for which universities assume responsibility should be relevant to educational goals. The Joint Statement does not advocate that community standards of decency and respectability be left to student group determination. However, it does insist that standards adopted by the university community be reconciled with an honest, objective search for a deeper understanding of man and the human condition.

The Joint Statement does not repudiate the diversity which exists among American colleges and universities as long as the particularities which characterize diverse cam-

13 Williamson, *op. cit.*, p. 309.

puses can be justified in terms of true educational goals. For instance, if a particular university can demonstrate that it is bringing to academe the unique insights of a particular religious background, it is anticipated that the principles of the Joint Statement will be implemented on such a campus in a manner that is compatible with this particular educational goal. The principles of the Statement would only require that such a university make adequate provision for a critical exchange of ideas with the rest of academe so that the right to learn with its complementary freedoms of inquiry and expression are not frustrated.

The Joint Statement seeks to guarantee freedom in the pursuit of truth through open dialogue, debate, and argument. Correspondingly, it strongly reinforces the right of each college and university to preserve the academic character of this dialogue. It is not a tenet of academic freedom, or of the Joint Statement, that truth will prevail in the midst of anarchy or chaos. The Statement recognizes that an academic community, no less than an individual person, can render itself incapable of perceiving truth through community bias or other community character deficiencies. The responsibility, therefore, of each academic community to develop a community character which is supportive of the pursuit of truth is defended by the Joint Statement. The Statement recognizes that the specifics of this character, along with the policies, standards, and safeguards that support it, will vary from campus to campus.

All who participated in the drafting of the Joint Statement, as well as those who participated in its endorsements, fully recognize that the Joint Statement does not speak the final word on student rights and freedoms. The endorsements all regard the Statement as a living document which needs a great deal of interpretation, study, and further clarification. Much of this deeper understanding will come as sincere efforts are made to implement the statement on

various and diverse campuses. The following commentary
is offered to assist in this understanding implementation.

D. COMMENTARY

Preamble

The Joint Statement begins by listing four reasons for the
existence of academic institutions: the transmission of
knowledge, the pursuit of truth, the development of students, and the welfare of society. Radical student groups
would today maintain that the development of students is
exclusively a concern of individual students. The responsibility of the university for students, as expressed in the
Statement, would involve their development only as members of a particular academic community. It is presumed
that development would include not only the achievement
of true academic goals but also an accommodation with
community standards, if these are necessary and appropriate to the achievement of the community's educational
goals. Whether or not, therefore, student development involves development of the "whole man," and precisely
what this involves depends on the stated *educational* goals
of each institution.

It is a time-honored tradition that one of the means by
which academic institutions provide for the general welfare
of society is by serving as critics of the larger society, its
values and its institutions. This particular function is little
understood in the United States where it has been taken for
granted until recent times that education served the larger
society almost exclusively by reinforcing existing societal
institutions and values. Student movements which are critical of long-accepted societal institutions and values must
be understood as exercising a legitimate, academic, critical

function—even when the focus of their attention turns on the educational system itself.

The Preamble recognizes that institutional procedures, policies, and general standards which are adopted to implement the spirit and principles of the Joint Statement will vary from campus to campus. It is firmly established in the endorsements (AAC, NASPA, and NAWDC) that the ultimate basis of these campus-to-campus variations will be the variety of educational goals which characterize colleges and universities in the United States. It follows that procedures, policies, and standards adopted on various campuses to assure freedom of inquiry and expression must ultimately be judged in terms of each institution's stated educational goals. It is assumed that the educational goals of a true university can always make adequate provision for the freedoms of inquiry and expression.

The Statement outlines "minimal standards of academic freedom" which it describes as "essential to any community of scholars." However, it cannot be assumed that every detailed prescription of the Joint Statement must be implemented on each campus in order to fulfill these minimal standards. The NASPA endorsement clearly distinguishes between *principles* which the Statement defines and *practices* which the Statement describes. Only the principles enunciated in the Joint Statement must be accepted as minimal standards of academic freedom. From campus to campus these minimal principles may be implemented in a variety of ways, possibly never precisely in accordance with the practices described in the Joint Statement. The principles are determined by the very nature of the academic enterprise. The autonomy and diversity of institutions are protected by providing that the principles may be implemented by a variety of means appropriate to the educational goals of each institution.

The Joint Statement presupposes that freedom of inquiry

and freedom of expression are indispensable to the attainment of its four stated goals. It might be added that adequate instruction, implied in the transmission of knowledge, is also indispensable to attain these goals. The academic community has a responsibility to develop in students the quality of making informed as well as free judgments. Moreover, it is presumed that the free inquiry and free expression of which the Joint Statement speaks will be ordered to "a sustained and independent search for truth." The academic community has a responsibility to protect free inquiry and free expression *only for this stated purpose*. Universities have no responsibility to protect free expression for campus power groupings which seek to impose their ideas on the community by denying to others the freedom upon which they insist for themselves.

The Joint Statement speaks of academic institutions as communities of scholars. Both terms in the expression are important. The *community* aspect of a university is strongly emphasized in the AAC, NASPA and NAWDC endorsements explicitly to repudiate the radical student view that the student sector of the academic institution should be autonomous. By using the term *scholars,* the Statement expresses an appropriate limitation of freedom in the academic community. The freedom to learn of which the Joint Statement speaks applies to students primarily, if not exclusively, in the context of students' developing the capacity for "a sustained and independent search for truth." Any freedom which would hinder the development of such a capacity is contrary to the ideals of an academic community.

The Joint Statement has been criticized because it does not explicitly outline the responsibilities of students in the community of scholars as it attempts explicitly to outline student rights and freedoms. There are several answers to this objection. First, generic reference is made to student responsibilities in the Preamble and elsewhere where responsibilities are imputed to *all* members of the community. But, more important, in delineating student rights and freedoms, corresponding responsibilities are implied. Every right and freedom involves a corresponding responsibility. The Joint Statement by no means urges that rights and freedoms of students be recognized without corresponding responsibilities being assumed. It might well be argued that by calling attention to the rights and freedoms of students, their responsibilities are being stressed.

I. FREEDOM OF ACCESS

That each university should be free to determine academic and behavioral standards which are necessary and appropriate to its specific educational goal is clearly stated in this first section of the Joint Statement. It is only required that such expectations be published in official literature readily available to all incoming students.[14]

II. IN THE CLASSROOM

Section II of the Joint Statement, like Section I, enunciates only principles. Neither section proposes practices by which the given principles might be implemented on various campuses. One of the practices suggested by students for implementing the principles outlined in this section involves a change from present grading practices to the pass-fail system. The more radical student movements suggest the abolition of all student grades on the basis that objective academic evaluation is impossible and subjective evaluation

[14] It is interesting to speculate how the principle enunciated in this section of the Joint Statement might be expanded to provide that education in the wide diversity of colleges and universities in the United States, private as well as public, should be made equally (financially) accessible to all students.

is too likely to be unfair. The Joint Statement defends the right of institutions to evaluate students both with respect to ability and character. However, these evaluations are to be regarded as confidential and normally are not to be passed on without the consent of the student. It is presumed that a healthy teacher-student relationship will incline a student, even in the classroom, to reveal a great deal of his inmost self. Teachers must regard such personal knowledge as highly confidential.

III. STUDENT RECORDS

The pervasive concern of students today with respect to confidentiality and privacy perhaps reflects the fact that our age is on the verge of developing total electronic recall. Problems arising from this concern for confidentiality recur throughout the document (Sections II, III, IV, A, and VI, B, 1). The American Council on Education has recently issued a "Statement on Confidentiality of Student Records" which perhaps better than anything else explains why this concern is so paramount in student minds today.

The maintenance of student records of all kinds, but especially those bearing on matters of belief and affiliation, inevitably creates a highly personal and confidential relationship. The mutual trust that this relationship implies is deeply involved in the educational process. Colleges acquire from students and other sources a great deal of private information about their enrollees for the basic purpose of facilitating their development as educated persons. This purpose is contravened when the material is made available to investigatory bodies without the student's permission. Thus, although a student may not require that his record be withdrawn, improperly altered or destroyed, he may appropriately expect his institution to release information about him only with his knowledge and consent.[15]

[15] "Statement on Confidentiality of Student Records," in *Chronicle of Higher Education,* August 23, 1967.

The Joint Statement provides that transcripts of academic records should contain only information about academic status. However, both the AAC and NASPA endorsements insist that transcripts also show any institutional action, such as suspension and expulsion for academic or disciplinary reasons, which affects a student's eligibility to re-register at the institution. If, and when, a student is readmitted to a school, it seems reasonable that the record of suspension (or expulsion) be removed from the transcript. It is generally agreed that records pertaining to health, psychological counseling, and discipline, other than the notations on a transcript mentioned above, are highly confidential. Such records should never be revealed without a student's knowledge and consent and even then not without proper interpretation.

IV. STUDENT AFFAIRS

The most difficult principles of the Joint Statement to implement on campuses will undoubtedly be those contained in the section on Student Affairs. This section is divided into four parts, three of which are closely associated: *A,* student associations; *B,* speakers invited to campus, and *D,* student publications. These three topics deal directly and immediately with the freedoms of inquiry and expression, the main concern of the document. Part *C* discusses a matter of equal importance, student participation in institutional government.

A problem arises in that the Joint Statement appears to concede to students an autonomy in the areas of student associations, invited speakers, and student publications. Interpretations of the Statement can be argued pro and con. The matter is clarified in the AAC, NASPA, and NAWDC endorsements. The third clarification of the AAC endorsement reads as follows:

Inasmuch as "the responsibility to secure and to respect general conditions conducive to the freedom to learn is shared by all members of the academic community," specific provisions of the Joint Statement, e.g., those for speakers, student organizations and student publications, should not be interpreted to concede absolute autonomy to the student sector when such provisions pertain to matters of proper concern to the academic community as a whole.

It should be noted that the clarification does not deny that students might be delegated an almost complete freedom in the areas concerned. The clarification specifies only that some matters in these areas could be "of proper concern to the community as a whole." In effect, the clarification reserves to the academic community as a whole *ultimate* decisions with respect to campus associations, speakers and student publications, it being presumed in the context of the Statement that the community will allow such freedoms in these areas as are compatible with an honest understanding of the right to learn. Further, it is implied that the community as a whole must justify limitations of student freedom in these areas in terms of specific educational goals and of community standards which are essential to the achievement of its goals.

The Joint Statement strongly urges—as a practice, not a principle—that university policies with respect to student affairs be carefully formulated in writing. This is as important for the community as it is for students. So many decisions in the area of student affairs must be made when "issues" arise, when emotions are high and when outside pressures are strong. Written policies, formulated when heads are cool and pressures non-existent, are more likely to reflect mature educational philosophy and, if well communicated, serve to protect whoever must make an unpopular decision in times of stress—and what decision is not unpopular in some quarter?

IV, A. FREEDOM OF ASSOCIATION

The precise freedom which "the community as a whole" should allow students to form student organizations gives rise to some very difficult problems. Speakers come and go. Editions of student publications are ephemeral. Modern students are usually sophisticated enough to judge critically speakers and publications. However, campus organizations are permanent, continually recruiting membership, continually striving to influence campus policies and standards, and, most important, continually working to implement their own specific goals in student life. Can an academic community as a whole approve a student organization which encourages acts that are diametrically opposed to ideals which the community feels are essential to its academic character? For example, is it conceivable that a student organization be allowed openly to solicit membership in a society which encourages the use of LSD and other dangerous drugs, if the community as a whole feels that the widespread use of such drugs would destroy its specific academic character? (Whether or not LSD is legal or illegal is quite beside the point.) If an academic community as a whole has the right to determine academic and behavioral standards which it considers necessary and appropriate to its educational goal, it would appear that it has a collateral right to deny official recognition to any student organization whose academic or behavioral practices cannot be reconciled with those standards.

This is not to deny that it is healthy in an academic community for even basic institutional values, commitments, and goals to be *intellectually* challenged. The educational institution must serve as its own critic, and somehow institutional criticism must be legitimatized even when this involves the official recognition of campus student organizations. However, intellectually to challenge institutional values, commitments, and goals is quite another thing from encouraging practices which do not academically challenge but by other means attempt to subvert institutional goals and standards.

Basically, the point at issue is the academic style or character of the academic institution. It might well be argued that a student organization which disrupts or circumvents the academic style or method of a university should be regarded as far more dangerous to the academic community than one which intellectually challenges university values, commitments and goals. In a community which maintains its true academic character, values, commitments and goals can only be clarified and strengthened by their being intellectually challenged.

Allowing for the distinction made by the NASPA endorsement between principles and practices in the Joint Statement, the various details outlined under the consideration of student organizations could be implemented on campus in a variety of ways. Domination by non-students is to be avoided in campus organizations. Paternalistic control by the institution through "trusted" moderators is likewise to be avoided. Where membership lists are not kept—and what institution can manage to keep membership lists up to date anyway—they cannot be demanded by outside agencies. A student's organizational affiliations are to be regarded as something personal, not a matter for public record.

IV, B. FREEDOM OF INQUIRY AND EXPRESSION

The right of individual students or of student organizations to express views by protests and demonstrations is to be respected. However, both the AAC and NASPA endorsements clarify the matter by insisting that non-interference with the "regular and essential operation of the institution" refers to *all* educational activities and practices outside as well as within the classroom. This is certainly intended to include all practices and activities associated with the operation of the institution—residence halls, book stores, food services, etc.—since the operation of the entire university complex is intended to provide an educational living experience for all facets of student life.

Once again the concern of the academic community for academic style or character is manifested in the endorsements. Four of the five sponsoring organizations explicitly condemn any type of protest or demonstration which disrupts the free expression of ideas. The AAUP resolution, already quoted, is most explicit on this point. A typical rule on demonstrations, such as can be reconciled with the principles of the Joint Statement, might read as follows:

Campus demonstrations are permitted provided they are conducted in an orderly manner and do not interfere with vehicular or pedestrian traffic, classes or other university activities and functions, and are not held within university buildings.[16]

The Joint Statement does not require that any student be allowed to invite any speaker to campus at any time. The principle involved is freedom of inquiry. Almost all institutions allow speakers to be invited to campus only by officially recognized student organizations. On most campuses there is no restriction whatsoever if speakers are invited to meet only with members of a particular student organization. A distinction is made on some campuses between student organizations inviting speakers to address members of the university community at a closed session and speakers invited to speak at meetings which are open to the public. In either case a particular speaker (or program) may be a "proper concern for the community as a

[16] Adapted from Stanford University statement on demonstrations.

whole" if community standards (necessary and appropriate for established educational goals) are at issue. The principle of "clear and present danger" can at times provide a further concern. It would be most irresponsible for an academic community to allow a student organization to invite a speaker to campus at a time when he might directly or indirectly induce violence in the larger society.

It is reasonable to expect, particularly on campuses where students have long been protected from ideas which are considered contrary to the ideals of American society, that students will seek to invite controversial speakers to campus as a challenge to traditional campus norms and sometimes simply to test the intellectual sincerity of administration and faculty. Freedom of inquiry is the principle at issue. Speakers invited under such circumstances, while satisfying a legitimate student interest and curiosity, normally exert little influence on student views. On the other hand, controversial speakers can have a very beneficial effect by focusing, and at times polarizing, campus discussion and argument. It should be kept in mind that students today hear and see controversial speakers regularly on television. They are generally far more familiar with controversial ideas and have usually developed a far more mature sophistication in forming critical judgments than faculty and administrators realize. A balanced program providing for controversial speakers can serve to make education relevant on a campus if the ideas presented are discussed later in curricular and co-curricular programs. Students today reasonably insist that they should not be protected from ideas. Where they are not protected they are quite anxious to discuss their reactions—even, and perhaps especially, with "people over thirty."

IV, C. STUDENT PARTICIPATION IN INSTITUTIONAL GOVERNMENT

It is one of the basic principles of the Joint Statement that students should be involved in institutional government. The principle is enunciated in the Preamble: policies and procedures should be developed at each institution within the framework of general standards *and with the broadest possible participation of members of the academic community*. In this section of the document the principle is specified: The student body should have clearly defined means to participate in the formulation and application of institutional policy affecting academic and student affairs. It is further indicated that the role of student government should be made explicit in both its general and specific responsibilities.

The AAC and NASPA endorsements clarify the principle of student participation in institutional government in the following words:

The participation of the student body "in the formulation and application of institutional policy affecting academic and student affairs" (Section IV, C) and "significant student participation" in the formulation of "standards of conduct" (Section VI, A) may involve a variety of activities, under methods appropriate to each campus, ranging from student discussion of proposed policy in committees, in organized agencies of student government, or through the student press to the more formal determination of policy by groups that include student members or, where and if delegated by appropriate authority, by groups that are composed only of students.

The AAC and NASPA position can by no means be understood to water down the Joint Statement principle. The intent is merely to specify, as practices, the variety of means by which students may represent their views in matters which are "a proper concern of the community as a whole."

In advocating student participation in institutional government, the Joint Statement once again expressly repudiates the radical student view that the student sector of the university community should be autonomous. The radical student view is sometimes expressed by students insisting that they have no responsibility to abide by any university rules which they themselves (unilaterally) have not made. The Joint Statement provides only that there should be "significant student participation" (VI, A) in the determination of standards of student conduct. On the other hand, the Statement does not deny the possibility that the community as a whole may wisely delegate to students far-reaching authority to regulate their own affairs in certain defined areas.

Universities today are obviously faced with serious problems in matters of institutional government. Student (and faculty) power is a reality. University administration charts and legal documents may show that the ultimate decision-making power rests completely and exclusively with the trustees, president, and other top administrative officers. However, the charts and legal documents may well serve only to certify what is increasingly referred to as "the illusion of final authority." Decisions are never made in a vacuum, as any university president will testify. Pressures by the public, alumni, parents, and fund sources, on the one hand, have to be reconciled with pressures from the academic community on the other. Moreover, a vocal minority in any group frequently presents views with a finality that is out of all proportion to the true sentiment of the group it claims to represent. All of these forces must be realistically balanced against the ideals of a true university in the decision-making process. Ultimate authority does, and indeed must, remain with the trustees and president. However, the realities of the situation are such that the trustees and president are well advised to exercise their authority through effective delegation and personally only after extensive consultation.

University government today requires a variety of skills not the least of which is a clear concept of the relationship between the student ideal expressed as the right to learn and the educational goals of a particular institution. While the student right to learn and institutional goals are not incompatible, their reconciliation will at times be a source of serious tension, especially in matters which are "a proper concern of the community as a whole." Student participation in institutional government serves to resolve these tensions by exposing students to the complexities involved in the decision-making process. Moreover, students bring to the process a peculiar competence which administration and faculty ignore only at their peril. Sometimes student insight expresses itself through a greater competence to ask penetrating questions than to provide ready answers. Penetrating student questions will often expose unfounded presumptions upon which poor decisions might otherwise have been made.

The following practices are suggested as means of implementing on various campuses the principle that students should participate in institutional government. First, *subsidiarity* must be observed. Effective authority must be delegated as completely as responsibility for the overall educational enterprise will allow. This means that a conscious effort must be made to see that individuals and groups, as far removed from the trustees and president as possible, are educated to the interrelatedness of everyday university decisions with ultimate educational goals.

Second, while strict nose-count democracy is not a reasonable form of university government, *democratic methods* do make sense in the academic community if the various university sectors are represented by respected members and the decision-making body is proportioned to the competence necessary for particular decisions. An academic community rightly insists that all sides to a question be adequately heard and represented to the final decision-making authority.

Third, the decision-making process, on whatever level, should always be *visible*. Members of an academic community (including faculty and fellow administrators) want to know, and have a right to know, precisely who—what individual or what committee—makes final decisions on particular issues.

Fourth, *time* is important. Decisions which are delayed interminably give the impression that those responsible for making the decision hope the problem can be pigeonholed or the issue forgotten. That important decisions should not be rushed is understandable, provided it is apparent that the delay is necessary for serious investigation and study. Tensions caused by delay can be greatly alleviated if the results of such investigation and study are reported regularly.

Fifth, *reasons* must be given with final decisions. Such a practice accords with the very nature of an academic community. By explaining decisions the decision-making process can be turned to educational advantage. Campus issues should provide a valuable circumstance by which students can be educated to the relation between particular decisions and community-respected goals.

Sixth, an absolute and irrevocable *finality should be avoided,* as far as possible, in making decisions. Rule and policy declarations which are declared to hold for all future times lead to needless later embarrassment or, because of a reluctance to rescind such decisions, to a continuation of rules and policies which have become anti-

quated and meaningless in contexts that were never anticipated. Firm decisions can be made "for the present" or
"for the foreseeable future," leaving the way open for
future discussion, developments, and possible well-advised
changes.

Last, utter and absolute *honesty* must characterize every
aspect of the decision-making process. There is no greater
frustration in any community than the feeling that those
responsible for making final decisions are not being forthright either during the investigatory process or in the reasons they provide for the decision they make.

IV, D. STUDENT PUBLICATIONS

In this particular section the Joint Statement appears
ambiguous. First, it recommends that student publications
be financially and legally independent of institutional control. Then, realizing that such a situation is not likely to
be implemented on a vast majority of campuses, the Statement recommends practices that will provide the freedom
which the Statement considers essential to student expression. In this latter instance the Statement provides for a
measure of ultimate, institutional control. Within a framework of written, clearly specified standards, complete freedom of expression is to be delegated to the student staff.
Moreover, the editor and staff are to be protected from
arbitrary removal or censure. Although student publications
are not to be precensored, prepublication leadership and
guidance by a faculty adviser as well as post-publication
review and critique would not be contrary to the principles
of the Joint Statement as long as such practices do not
interfere with editorial freedom.

The specter is frequently raised of a university, as publisher, being sued for libel for injudicious statements by

student editors. The Statement appears to treat this matter with an almost cavalier attitude. Actually, although such legal action remains in the realm of the possible, the likelihood of an offended party's being successful in such a suit is not very great where precensorship is explicitly and formally renounced. Law with respect to libel actions increasingly favors freedom of the press. Moreover, the practice of not precensoring student publications is so widespread and educationally defensible that there is little likelihood that any court would hold a university negligent if it does not precensor student publications.

The Joint Statement does not take up the difficult problems related to the designation of student editors. Campus publications can lose their freedom if editors and staff are allowed to perpetuate themselves and their views. Since student publications are of such vital concern to the academic community as a whole, perhaps the best way to handle the appointment of new editors is through a publications board which represents all segments of the university community.

V. OFF-CAMPUS FREEDOM OF STUDENTS

According to more radical student views, student conduct off campus—indeed, outside the classroom—is not a legitimate concern of the university. The Joint Statement makes no declaration in this matter. However, at least one important recent court decision substantiates the position that the conduct of students off campus is not only a matter of legitimate university concern but can be a matter of considerable university responsibility.[17]

This section of the Joint Statement is concerned with

[17] Goldberg v. Regents of University of California, 57 Calif. Reporter, 463, 473, April, 1967.

something quite different. At issue is the right of students while off campus to exercise their civil rights without being in jeopardy of university disciplinary action. The principle is asserted that such student acts, even acts of civil disobedience, are not in themselves a legitimate university concern. In such cases the university should neither punish students nor interfere with their having to suffer the full civil consequences of their conduct. The Statement reacts to the situation which prevailed in many, particularly southern, schools where students were peremptorily dismissed or otherwise punished for exercising their rights as citizens by taking part in civil rights demonstrations off campus.

Another basic consideration proposed by the Joint Statement is that the university ordinarily should not act as an arm or agent of civil law-enforcement agencies, especially by reinforcing civil penalties with university censures when the civil offense has no relation to university standards as an academic community. Again, neither should students be protected from the full effects of civil censure for their offenses against civil society. With the understanding that a particular student act might at times be the legitimate, but separate, concern of both the civil and university communities, it is considered best that the two jurisdictions be kept clearly distinct. In general, the university should concern itself with civil law violations by students off campus only when

such conduct calls into question the student's membership in the educational community either because he has grossly violated elemental standards of behavior requisite to the maintenance of an educational community or because his continued presence would adversely affect the ability of others to pursue their educational goal.[18]

[18] "Sindler Commission Report," *The Cornell Daily Sun*, Wednesday, October 4, 1967.

VI. PROCEDURAL STANDARDS IN DISCIPLINARY PROCEEDINGS

The Joint Statement has been strongly criticized for the excessive legalism of the practices, not principles, it outlines for "procedural due process in cases requiring a high degree of formality." University officers responsible for campus disciplinary procedures fear that the practices recommended by the Statement establish an adversary relationship between the institution and its students which precludes mutual confidence and trust. Many university officers feel that the Joint Statement does not recognize that a majority of disciplinary cases, even those which initially might appear to merit suspension or dismissal, are terminated in the dean's office with effective educational guidance.

The AAC and NASPA endorsements react strongly to the detailed prescriptions of the Joint Statement.

A committee for joint interpretation should accept as one of its primary responsibilities an exploration for alternative procedures which, while assuring "fair play" and making adequate provision for "procedural due process," would be more appropriate to an academic community (Dixon vs. Alabama Board of Education) and more adaptable to educational goals by encouraging a relationship of mutual respect and trust especially in cases where "misconduct may result in serious penalties."

The basic principle involved in this whole matter is "fair play" in *all* disciplinary proceedings. The requirements of "fair play" as currently required by the courts are outlined in the third introductory paragraph of this section. Some of the presciptions incorporated under Hearing Committee Procedures go beyond present court requirements.

The practice of allowing a student to have the assistance and guidance of an adviser during formal university disciplinary proceedings is widespread today. It is important, therefore, to call attention to the fact that the word "adviser" is used in the Joint Statement (VI, D, 3) rather than the word "counsel" which had been suggested. The word "adviser," it was felt, explains better the practice of most schools which, in order to assure an academic character in campus disciplinary hearings, requires that the adviser be a member (in some places a tenured faculty member) of the academic community.

A final word might be said about university rules. In what detail need behavioral expectations be spelled out in student rules? Two extremes are to be avoided. Vague statements which do not provide definite norms and which can be arbitrarily interpreted are obviously unacceptable. On the other hand, precise and detailed lists of student offenses with penalties specified for each violation are not required. A reasonable explanation of behavioral expectations, as specified by the Joint Statement, is all that is necessary.

CONCLUSION

The objection has been raised that the Joint Statement is already out of date. It is argued that the Statement presupposes conditions of education which are a thing of the past—a stable academic community with its own respected academic style providing freedoms which are appropriate to its traditional character. It is felt that these conditions, drawn in part from an ivory-tower concept of university life, simply will not prevail in the days ahead and that the principles of the Joint Statement will have little application to the "era of confrontation" which already is developing.

In the years ahead, particularly on large, highly impersonal campuses, it is reasonable to presume that radical student ambitions will not be satisfied by providing students a minority representation on university policy-forming committees. Some students will feel, it is feared, increasing frustration as they perceive their ineffectiveness directly to control or adequately to influence the decision-making processes. Tensions will consequently build to the breaking point. Radical students will perceive that power, exercised in a variety of extra-legal forms, brings results that cooperation within the established academic style could never achieve.

It is probably inevitable that on many campuses the pendulum will swing to and fro in response to power actions and reactions by various groupings. In such a circumstance the function of the Joint Statement may be to provide norms which will be considered academically responsible by a strong majority of the university community. Moreover, it must be remembered that the Joint Statement makes no claim to speak the final word on student rights and freedoms. The Statement is intended to be a living document subject to further understandings and clarifications. Perhaps the swinging of the pendulum for a time will be necessary to clarify these understandings on many campuses.

In its basic thrust the Joint Statement presumes one particular educational development as inevitable. Due to the extensive social revolution the world is currently experiencing the Statement anticipates that students, foreseeing the responsibilities they will be required to assume in the evolving society, will insist on assuming an ever-increasing responsibility for their own self-development.

Anticipating this trend, the Joint Statment asserts quite strongly that the academic community as a whole cannot abdicate its own share of responsibility for the development of students. Well aware of the tensions that are certain to arise on campuses as a result of this shared responsibility, the Joint Statement attempts to provide fundamental principles according to which these tensions can be resolved with academic integrity.

II

Documents

A. Joint Statement on Rights and Freedoms of Students *

PREAMBLE

ACADEMIC INSTITUTIONS EXIST for the transmission of knowledge, the pursuit of truth, the development of students, and the general well-being of society. Free inquiry and free expression are indispensable to the attainment of these goals. As members of the academic community, students should be encouraged to develop the capacity for critical judgment and to engage in a sustained and independent search for truth. Institutional procedures for achieving these purposes may vary from campus to campus, but the minimal standards of aca-

* Previously published in *College and University Business*, September, 1967, pp. 78-81. Reprinted by permission.

demic freedom of students outlined below are essential to any community of scholars.

Freedom to teach and freedom to learn are inseparable facets of academic freedom. The freedom to learn depends upon appropriate opportunities and conditions in the classroom, on the campus, and in the larger community. Students should exercise their freedom with responsibility.

The responsibility to secure and to respect general conditions conducive to the freedom to learn is shared by all members of the academic community. Each college and university has a duty to develop policies and procedures which provide and safeguard this freedom. Such policies and procedures should be developed at each institution within the framework of general standards and with the broadest possible participation of the members of the academic community. The purpose of this statement is to enumerate the essential provisions for student freedom to learn.

I. FREEDOM OF ACCESS TO HIGHER EDUCATION

The admissions policies of each college and university are a matter of institutional choice provided that each college and university makes clear the characteristics and expectations of students which it considers relevant to success in the institution's program. While church-related institutions may give admission preference to students of their own persuasion, such a preference should be clearly and publicly stated. Under no circumstances should a student be barred from admission to a particular institution on the basis of race. Thus, within the limits of its facilities, each college and university should be open to all students who are qualified according to its admission standards. The facilities and services of a college should be open to all of its enrolled students, and institutions should use their influence to secure equal access for all students to public facilities in the local community.

II. IN THE CLASSROOM

The professor in the classroom and in conference should encourage free discussion, inquiry, and expression. Student performance should be evaluated solely on an academic basis, not on opinions or conduct in matters unrelated to academic standards.

A. *Protection of Freedom of Expression.* Students should be free to take reasoned exception to the data or views offered in any course of study and to reserve judgment about matters of opinion, but they are responsible for learning the content of any course of study for which they are enrolled.

B. *Protection Against Improper Academic Evaluation.* Students should have protection through orderly procedures against prejudiced or capricious academic evaluation. At the same time, they are responsible for maintaining standards of academic performance established for each course in which they are enrolled.

C. *Protection Against Improper Disclosure.* Information about student views, beliefs, and political associations which professors acquire in the course of their work as instructors, advisers, and counselors should be considered confidential. Protection against improper disclosure is a serious professional obligation. Judgments of ability and character may be provided under appropriate circumstances, normally with the knowledge or consent of the student.

III. STUDENT RECORDS

Institutions should have a carefully considered policy as to the information which should be part of a student's permanent educational record and as to the conditions of its disclosure. To minimize the risk of improper discolsure, academic and disciplinary records should be separate, and the conditions of access to each should be set forth in an explicit policy statement. Transcripts of academic records should contain only information about academic status. Information from disciplinary or counseling files should not be available to unauthorized persons on campus, or to any person off campus without the express consent of the student involved except under legal compulsion or in cases where the safety of persons or property is involved. No records should be kept which reflect the political activities or beliefs of students. Provision should also be made for periodic routine destruction of non-current disciplinary records. Administrative staff and faculty members should respect confidential information about students which they acquire in the course of their work.

IV. STUDENT AFFAIRS

In student affairs, certain standards must be maintained if the freedom of students is to be preserved.

A. *Freedom of Association.* Students bring to the campus a variety of interests previously acquired and develop many new interests as members of the academic community. They should be free to organize and join associations to promote their common interests.

1. The membership, policies, and actions of a student organization usually will be determined by vote of only those persons who hold bona fide membership in the college or university community.

2. Affiliation with an extramural organization should not of itself disqualify a student organization from institutional recognition.

3. If campus advisers are required each organization should be free to choose its own adviser, and institutional recognition should not be withheld or withdrawn solely because of the inability of a student organization to secure an adviser. Campus advisers may advise organizations in the exercise of responsibility, but they should not have the authority to control the policy of such organizations.

4. Student organizations may be required to submit a statement of purpose, criteria for membership, rules of procedures, and a current list of officers. They should not be required to submit a membership list as a condition of institutional recognition.

5. Campus organizations, including those affiliated with an extramural organization, should be open to all students without respect to race, creed, or national origin, except for religious qualifications which may be required by organizations whose aims are primarily sectarian.

B. *Freedom of Inquiry and Expression*

1. Students and student organizations should be free to examamine and discuss all questions of interest to them, and to express opinions publicly and privately. They should always be free to support causes by orderly means which do not disrupt the regular and essential operation of the institution. At the same time, it should be made clear to the academic and the larger community that in their public expressions or demonstrations students or student organizations speak only for themselves.

2. Students should be allowed to invite and to hear any person of their own choosing. Those routine procedures required by an institution before a guest speaker is invited to appear on campus should be designed only to insure that there is orderly scheduling of facilities and adequate preparation for the event, and that the occasion is conducted in a manner appropriate to an academic community. The institutional control of campus facilities should not be used as a device of censorship. It should be made clear to the academic and larger community that sponsorship of guest speakers does not necessarily imply approval or endorsement of the views expressed, either by the sponsoring group or the institution.

C. *Student Participation in Institutional Government.* As constituents of the academic community, students should be free, individually and collectively, to express their views on issues of institutional policy and on matters of general interest to the student body. The student body should have clearly defined means to participate in the formulation and application of institutional policy affecting academic and student affairs. The role of the student government and both its general and specific responsibilities should be made explicit, and the actions of the student government within the areas of its jurisdiction should be reviewed only through orderly and prescribed procedures.

D. *Student Publications.* Student publications and the student press are a valuable aid in establishing and maintaining an atmosphere of free and responsible discussion and of intellectual exploration on the campus. They are a means of bringing student concerns to the attention of the faculty and the institutional authorities and of formulating student opinion on various issues on the campus and in the world at large.

Whenever possible the student newspaper should be an independent corporation financially and legally separate from the university. Where financial and legal autonomy is not possible, the institution, as the publisher of student publications, may have to bear the legal responsibility for the contents of the publications. In the delegation of editorial responsibility to students the institution must provide sufficient editorial freedom and financial autonomy for the student publications to maintain their integrity of purpose as vehicles for free inquiry and free expression in an academic community.

Institutional authorities, in consultation with students and faculty, have a responsibility to provide written clarification of the role of the student publications, the standards to be used in their evaluation, and the limitations on external control of their operation. At the same time, the editorial freedom of student editors and managers entails corollary responsibilities to be governed by the canons of responsible journalism, such as the avoidance of libel, indecency, undocumented allegations, attacks on personal integrity, and the techniques of harassment and innuendo. As safeguards for the editorial freedom of student publications the following provisions are necessary:

1. The student press should be free of censorship and advance approval of copy, and its editors and managers should be free to develop their own editorial policies and news coverage.

2. Editors and managers of student publications should be protected from arbitrary suspension and removal because of student, faculty, administrative, or public disapproval of editorial policy or content. Only for proper and stated causes should editors and managers be subject to removal and then by orderly and prescribed procedures. The agency responsible for the appointment of editors and managers should be the agency responsible for their removal.

3. All university published and financed student publications

should explicitly state on the editorial page that the opinions there expressed are not necessarily those of the college, university or student body.

V. OFF-CAMPUS FREEDOM OF STUDENTS

A. *Exercise of Rights of Citizenship.* College and university students are both citizens and members of the academic community. As citizens, students should enjoy the same freedom of speech, peaceful assembly, and right of petition that other citizens enjoy and, as members of the academic community, they are subject to the obligations which accrue to them by virtue of this membership. Faculty members and administrative officials should insure that institutional powers are not employed to inhibit such intellectual and personal development of students as is often promoted by their exercise of the rights of citizenship both on and off campus.

B. *Institutional Authority and Civil Penalties.* Activities of students may upon occasion result in violation of law. In such cases, institutional officials should be prepared to apprise students of sources of legal counsel and may offer other assistance. Students who violate the law may incur penalties prescribed by civil authorities, but institutional authority should never be used merely to duplicate the function of general laws. Only where the institution's interests as an academic community are distinct and clearly involved should the special authority of the institution be asserted. The student who incidentally violates institutional regulations in the course of his off-campus activity, such as those relating to class attendance, should be subject to no greater penalty than would normally be imposed. Institutional action should be independent of community pressure.

VI. PROCEDURAL STANDARDS IN DISCIPLINARY PROCEEDINGS

In developing responsible student conduct, disciplinary proceedings play a role substantially secondary to example, counseling, guidance, and admonition. At the same time, educational institutions have a duty and the corollary disciplinary powers to protect their educational purpose through the setting of standards of scholarship and conduct for the students who attend

them and through the regulation of the use of institutional facilities. In the exceptional circumstances when the preferred
means fail to resolve problems of student conduct, proper
procedural safeguards should be observed to protect the student from the unfair imposition of serious penalties.

The administration of discipline should guarantee procedural
fairness to an accused student. Practices in disciplinary cases
may vary in formality with the gravity of the offense and the
sanctions which may be applied. They should also take into
account the presence or absence of an Honor Code, and the
degree to which the institutional officials have direct acquaint-
ance with student life, in general, and with the involved student and the circumstances of the case in particular. The
jurisdictions of faculty or student judicial bodies, the disciplinary responsibilities of institutional officials and the regular
disciplinary procedures, including the student's right to appeal
a decision, should be clearly formulated and communicated in
advance. Minor penalties may be assessed informally under
prescribed procedures.

In all situations, procedural fair play requires that the student be informed of the nature of the charges against him, that
he be given a fair opportunity to refute them, that the institution
not be arbitrary in its actions, and that there be provision for
appeal of a decision. The following are recommended as proper
safeguards in such proceedings when there are no Honor Codes
offering comparable guarantees.

A. *Standards of Conduct Expected of Students.* The institution
has an obligation to clarify those standards of behavior which
it considers essential to its educational mission and its community life. These general behavioral expectations and the
resultant specific regulations should represent a reasonable
regulation of student conduct but the student should be as free
as possible from imposed limitations that have no direct relevance to his education. Offenses should be as clearly defined
as possible and interpreted in a manner consistent with the
aforementioned principles of relevancy and reasonableness. Disciplinary proceedings should be instituted only for violations of
standards of conduct formulated with significant student participation and published in advance through such means as a
student handbook or a generally available body of institutional
regulations.

B. *Investigation of Student Conduct.*

1. Except under extreme emergency circumstances, premises occupied by students and the personal possessions of students should not be searched unless appropriate authorization has been obtained. For premises such as residence halls controlled by the institution, an appropriate and responsible authority should be designated to whom application should be made before a search is conducted. The application should specify the reasons for the search and the objects or information sought. The student should be present, if possible, during the search. For premises not controlled by the institution, the ordinary requirements for lawful search should be followed.

2. Students detected or arrested in the course of serious violations of institutional regulations, or infractions of ordinary law, should be informed of their rights. No form of harassment should be used by institutional representatives to coerce admissions of guilt or information about conduct of other suspected persons.

C. *Status of Student Pending Final Action.* Pending action on the charges, the status of a student should not be altered, or his right to be present on the campus and to attend classes suspended, except for reasons relating to his physical or emotional safety and well-being, or for reasons relating to the safety and well-being of students, faculty, or university property.

D. *Hearing Committee Procedures.* When the misconduct may result in serious penalties and if the student questions the fairness of disciplinary action taken against him, he should be granted, on request, the privilege of a hearing before a regularly constituted hearing committee. The following suggested hearing committee procedures satisfy the requirements of "procedural due process" in situations requiring a high degree of formality:

1. The hearing committee should include faculty members or students, or, if regularly included or requested by the accused, both faculty and student members. No member of the hearing committee who is otherwise interested in the particular case should sit in judgment during the proceeding.

2. The student should be informed, in writing, of the reasons for the proposed disciplinary action with sufficient particularity, and in sufficient time, to insure opportunity to prepare for the hearing.

3. The student appearing before the hearing committee should have the right to be assisted in his defense by an adviser of his choice.

4. The burden of proof should rest upon the officials bringing the charge.

5. The student should be given an opportunity to testify and to present evidence and witnesses. He should have an opportunity to hear and question adverse witnesses. In no case should the committee consider statements against him unless he has been advised of their content and the names of those who made them, and unless he has been given an opportunity to rebut unfavorable inferences which might otherwise be drawn.

6. All matters upon which the decision may be based must be introduced into evidence at the proceeding before the Hearing Committee. The decision should be based solely upon such matter. Improperly acquired evidence should not be admitted.

7. In the absence of a transcript, there should be both a digest and a verbatim record, such as a tape recording, of the hearing.

8. The decision of the Hearing Committee should be final, subject only to the student's right of appeal to the President or ultimately to the governing board of the institution.

B. Resolution Adopted by the AAUP Council, October 29, 1967,

as it officially endorsed in a separate resolution the

Joint Statement on Rights and Freedoms of Students

THE AMERICAN ASSOCIATION OF UNIVERSITY PROFESSORS and the academic community have long stressed the fundamental principle set forth in the 1940 *Statement of Principles on Academic Freedom and Tenure* that "The common good depends upon the free search for truth and its free exposition." Universities and colleges are dependent for their very life on the maintenance of this principle within their walls. The Council of the American Association of University Professors has again asserted this principle at its meeting of October 28, 1967.

The Council also approved the *Joint Statement on Rights and Freedoms of Students,* which affirms that "Free inquiry and free expression are indispensable to the attainment of the goals" of academic institutions. The *Joint Statement* emphasizes that "the responsibility to secure and to respect general conditions conducive to the freedom to learn is shared by all members of the academic community" and develops other implications of these principles. The *Statement* notes that students should "be free to support causes by an orderly means which do not disrupt the regular and essential operation of the institution."

In view of some recent events, the Council *deems it important to state its conviction that action by individuals or groups to prevent speakers* invited to the campus from speaking, *to disrupt the operations* of the institutions in the course of demonstrations, *or to obstruct and restrain other members of the academic community* and campus visitors by physical force is destructive of the pursuit of learning and of a free society. ALL COMPONENTS of the academic community are under a strong obligation to protect its processes from these tactics.

C. Endorsement of the Joint Statement on Rights and Freedoms of Students
by the Jesuit Educational Association Commission on Colleges and Universities, January 14, 1968

WE HAVE EXAMINED the Joint Statement on the Rights and Freedoms of Students and endorse its spirit and principle. We affirm that the purpose of an academic institution is "the transmission of knowledge, the pursuit of truth, the development of students, and the general well-being of society." We agree that "institutional procedures for achieving these purposes may vary from campus to campus" because of the wide diversity of educational goals which characterizes college and university education in our country.

In particular, we are pleased that the Joint Statement articulates so explicitly that a college or university is a "community of scholars" who share the responsibility for the proper functioning of the institution in the pursuit of its educational goal. If we have reservations with regard to some specific recommendations in the document, it is only because we feel that some of its provisions might be interpreted to concede an autonomy to the student sector with respect to matters which are a legitimate concern of the academic community as a whole.

D. AAC Resolution *re* Joint Statement
Accepted by AAC on January 17, 1968

WHEREAS representatives of the Association of American Colleges have participated in extended discussions with representatives of the American Association of University Professors, the National Association of Student Personnel Administrators, the National Association of Women Deans and Counselors, and the United States National Student Association concerning the rights and freedoms of students and also, at various stages in the discussion, concerning the responsibilities of students and the participation of students in institutional governance, and

WHEREAS within that context of discussion and concern representatives of these five associations have together drafted a Joint Statement on Rights and Freedoms of Students which sets forth important principles, and

WHEREAS the Joint Statement presents principles on the basis of which interpretation of higher education should spell out the means by which appropriate features of the freedom of students to learn may be provided on each campus,

THEREFORE, be it resolved that the Association of American Colleges endorses the Joint Statement with the following explicit understandings for clarification:

1. That, as agreed in the drafting process, the several national associations endorsing the Joint Statement will set up machinery for continuing joint interpretation of the principles and suggested procedures described in the Statement, and that the development of any machinery for mediating disputes, investigating complaints, or resolving conflicts of rights in the university community, will be the product of joint consultation;

2. That the formulation of detailed procedures for securing the student's freedom to learn is the responsibility of each institution, must be in harmony with the educational purpose of the institution, and may therefore indeed "vary from campus to campus" (Statement Preamble);

3. That inasmuch as "the responsibility to secure and to respect

general conditions conducive to the freedom to learn is shared by all members of the academic community," specific provisions of the Joint Statement, e.g., those for speakers, student organizations and student publications, should not be interpreted to concede absolute autonomy to the student sector when such provisions pertain to matters of proper concern to the academic community as a whole;

4. That the provision of the Statement on Student Records (Section III) that "transcripts of academic records should contain only information about academic status" is to be understood as permitting the recording of any institutional action, such as suspension and expulsion for academic or disciplinary reasons, which affects a student's eligibility to re-register at the institution;

5. That the "regular and essential operation of the institution" which is not to be disrupted by student action (Section IV B 1) and the discussion which is concerned with avoiding limitations "not relevant" to the student's "education" (Section VI A) are both to be understood in the context of the whole educational mission of the institution, including as relevant its educational activities and practices that pertain outside as well as within the classroom;

6. That the participation of the student body "in the formulation and application of institutional policy affecting academic and student affairs" (Section IV C) and "significant student participation" in the formulation of "standards of conduct" (Section VI A) may involve a variety of activities, under methods appropriate to each campus, ranging from student discussion of proposed policy in committees, in organized agencies of student government, or through the student press to the more formal determination of policy by groups that include student members or, where and if delegated by appropriate authority, by groups that are composed only of students;

7. That restraints on the assertion of "the special authority of the institution" (Section V B) do not exclude institutional action merely because a student has also violated a civil statute;

8. That a committee for joint interpretation should accept as one of its primary responsibilities an exploration for alterna-

tive procedures which, while assuring "fair play" and making adequate provision for "procedural due process," would be more appropriate to an academic community (Dixon vs. Alabama Board of Education) and more adaptable to educational goals by encouraging a relationship of mutual respect and trust especially in cases where "misconduct may result in serious penalties";

9. That the Association of American Colleges joins with the Council of the American Association of University Professors in "its conviction" that, in the exercise of freedom "to support causes by orderly means" (Statement, Section IV B), "action by individuals or groups to prevent speakers invited to the campus from speaking, to disrupt the operations of the institution in the course of demonstrations, or to obstruct and restrain other members of the academic community and campus visitors by physical force is destructive of the pursuit of learning and of a free society" and in the Council's further statement "that all components of the academic community are under a strong obligation to protect its processes from these tactics" (Council Resolution, October 29, 1967); and

10. That the Association of American Colleges stands ready to work constructively with other interested associations in the further formulation of the student responsibilities which freedom entails and in the further delineation of the effective means by which students can best contribute to planning, decision-making, and other processes in the governance of colleges and universities for the mutual welfare of individuals, institutions, and a free society.

E. NASPA Endorsement of Joint Statement, April 2, 1968

WHEREAS, the National Association of Student Personnel Administrators has participated in extended study and discussion with representatives of the Association of American Colleges, the American Association of University Professors, the National Association of Women Deans and Counselors and the United States National Student Association concerning the rights and freedoms of students, their responsibilities and their participation in institutional governance, and

WHEREAS, as a result of that study and discussion representatives of the five cooperating associations have drafted a *Joint Statement on Rights and Freedoms of Students* which defines important principles and describes possible practices;

THEREFORE, be it resolved that the National Association of Student Personnel Administrators endorse the *Joint Statement* with the following understandings and interpretations:

UNDERSTANDINGS

1. That, in accord with the spirit and agreement of the joint drafting committee that "the responsibility to secure and respect general conditions conducive to the freedom to learn is shared by all members of the academic community":

   a. The several national associations endorsing the *Joint Statement* will establish a *committee for continuing interpretation of the document.* In accord with this understanding, the development of any procedures for mediating disputes, investigating complaints or resolving conflicts will be the product of joint consultation. In addition, a primary responsibility of the committee will be to develop alternative methods to assure procedural due process appropriate to the academic community in a relationship of mutual trust and respect.

   b. Specific provisions of the *Joint Statement* are understood as not endorsing any designation of absolute autonomy to any sector of the academic community, but instead as promoting a community approach to all matters of proper concern to that community as a whole.

2. That implementation of the *Joint Statement* is the responsibility of each institution, must be in harmony with its educational purposes, and may, therefore, "vary from campus to campus" (Statement Preamble).

3. That as students exercise the rights and freedoms defined in the *Joint Statement* they will do so with concomitant responsibility as a prerequisite for achievement of the educational objectives involved.

INTERPRETATIONS

1. That the provision in Section III regarding Student Records that "transcripts of academic records should contain only information about academic status" is to be interpreted to permit the recording of *any* institutional action which affects a student's eligibility to re-register at the institution (e.g., suspension or expulsion for academic or disciplinary reasons).

2. That the "regular and essential operation of the institution" which is not to be disrupted by student action (Section IV B 1) and the freedom from limitations "not relevant" to the student's "education" (Section VI A) are both to be interpreted in the context of the educational mission of the institution, including as relevant its educational activities outside as well as within the classroom.

3. That the participation of students "in the formulation and application of institutional policy affecting academic and student affairs" (Section IV C) and "significant student participation" in the formulation of "standards of conduct" (Section VI A) may involve a variety of methods appropriate to each campus. These may include, but are not limited to: student *discussion* of proposed policy in committees, in organized agencies of student government or in the student press; more formal *determination* of policy by groups that include student members, or, where appropriate, by groups that are composed only of students, and

BE IT FURTHER RESOLVED, that the National Association of Student Personnel Administrators advise all interested associations that it stands ready to participate fully in the further formulation of desirable student freedoms to learn and opportunities for appropriate participation as members of the academic community in institutional governance.

F. NAWDC Convention, Chicago, Illinois, April 3–7, 1968
Report of the Committee on Resolutions

WHEREAS, NAWDC throughout its history has expressed concern for the educational opportunities for all students,

WHEREAS, NAWDC has continually reaffirmed the association's respect for the rights, freedom and dignity of the individual and has spoken repeatedly for nondiscrimination in all forms and procedures,

WHEREAS, NAWDC has concern for the breadth of the educational mission which encompasses all aspects of student learning,

THEREFORE, Be it resolved that NAWDC endorses *The Joint Statement on Rights and Freedoms of Students,* formulated by the following organizations:

American Association of Colleges
United States National Student Association
National Association of Student Personnel Administrators
National Association of Women Deans and Counselors
American Association of University Professors.

BE IT FURTHER RESOLVED, that the interpretation of the Statement's principles and procedures be a continuing joint interpretation by the National Associations formulating the Statement.

BE IT FURTHER RESOLVED, that the implementation of the Statement's principles and procedures, as interpreted through joint consultation of the Associations, be understood to be a continuing process to be worked out on each campus according to the educational purposes of that particular institution.

BE IT FURTHER RESOLVED, that NAWDC endorses a community approach and that no sector of that community have autonomy in such matters.

FURTHERMORE, BE IT RESOLVED, that NAWDC joins with the Council of the American Association of University Professors in "its conviction" that, in the exercise of freedom "to support causes by orderly means" (Statement, Section IV B), "action by individuals or groups to prevent speakers invited to the campus from speaking, to disrupt the operations of the institution in the course of demonstrations, or to obstruct and restrain other members of the academic community and campus visitors by physical force is destructive of the pursuit of learning and of a free society" and in the Council's further statement that "all components of the academic community are under a strong obligation to protect its processes from these tactics" (Council Resolution, October 29, 1967).